John R. Pescosolido
Professor Emeritus
Central Connecticut State University
New Britain, Connecticut

Reviewers

Maria Driend
Literacy Coordinator
Cooperative Education Services
Trumbull, Connecticut

Terese D'Amico
Gifted Education Specialist for Grades 3–6
Thomas Jefferson Magnet School
Euclid City Schools
Euclid, Ohio

Patricia D'Amore
Assistant Literacy Coordinator
Cooperative Educational Services
Trumbull, Connecticut

Dr. Donna Ronzone
Principal and Director of Special Education
Briggs Elementary School District
Santa Paula, California

STECK-VAUGHN
ELEMENTARY · SECONDARY · ADULT · LIBRARY

A Harcourt Company

www.steck-vaughn.com

Acknowledgments

Editorial Director Stephanie Muller
Senior Editor Amanda Sperry
Assistant Editor Julie M. Smith
Associate Director of Design Cynthia Ellis
Senior Design Manager Cynthia Hannon
Designer Deborah Diver
Media Researcher Sarah Fraser
Editorial Development, Design, and Production The Quarasan Group, Inc.
Cover Illustration Doug Henry
Senior Technical Advisor Alan Klemp

PHOTO CREDITS

3 ©Raymond Gehman/Corbis; 5 ©Jonathan Blair/Corbis; 6 © Pictor International, Ltd./ PictureQuest; 8 ©SuperStock, Inc.; 13 ©Digital Studios; 14 ©Corbis/PictureQuest; 16 top (t) ©Andre Jenny/Focus Group/PictureQuest; bottom (b) ©Stephen J. Krasemann/DRK Photo; 17 top left (tl) ©Raymond Gehman/Corbis; top right (tr) ©Corbis; (b) ©Corbis; 18 (t) ©Corbis; (b) ©PhotoDisc, Inc.; 20 ©Becky Luigart-Stayner/Corbis; 21 ©PhotoDisc, Inc.; 24 ©Joe Atlas/Artville; 26 ©MetaTools; 31 (l) ©Gary Conner/Index Stock Imagery/PictureQuest; (r) ©David Young-Wolff/PhotoEdit, Inc.; 32 ©Quarasan; 34-36 ©The Granger Collection, New York; 37 ©PhotoDisc, Inc.; 39 ©Digital Studios; 41 ©David Young-Wolff/PhotoEdit, Inc.; 42 ©PhotoDisc, Inc.; 45 (l) ©PhotoDisc, Inc.; (r) ©Eyewire, Inc.; 46-47 ©PhotoDisc, Inc.; 48 ©Wood Sabold/International Stock; 52 ©SuperStock, Inc.; 53 ©Digital Studios; 54 ©Warren Faidley/International Stock; 56 ©Wayne R. Bilenduke/Stone; 58 ©George D. Lepp/Stone; 60 ©Corbis; 62 (t) ©George McCarthy/Corbis; (b) ©Robert Gill/Papilio/Corbis; 63 ©Jeffrey L. Rotman/Corbis; 64 ©George McCarthy/Corbis; 66 ©Steve Bly/International Stock; 67 ©SuperStock, Inc.; 70 ©Bo Zaunders/The Stock Market; 72 ©David Young-Wolff/PhotoEdit, Inc.; 73 ©Corbis; 74 (Canadian penny) ©Quarasan; (U.S. penny) ©MetaTools; 75 ©David Young-Wolff/PhotoEdit, Inc.; 76 ©Charles Gupton/The Stock Market; 80 ©MetaTools; 81 ©James D'Addio/The Stock Market; 82 ©Frank Siteman/PhotoEdit, Inc.; 86 ©Michael Newman/PhotoEdit, Inc.; 88 ©Ric Ergenbright/Corbis; 94 ©Tom Bean/Stone; 95 ©Corel Corporation; 97 (background) ©Cartesia; 98 ©Flip Schulke/Corbis; 100 ©Harold E. Wilson/Animals Animals; 105 ©PhotoDisc, Inc.; 107 (t) ©PhotoDisc, Inc.; (b) ©Corbis; 109 ©SuperStock, Inc.; 110 ©Robert Ginn/PhotoEdit, Inc.; 112 ©Stan Osolinski/Stock Market; 113 (t) ©PhotoDisc, Inc.; (b) ©Kevin Schafer/Corbis; 114 (t) ©Stan Osolinski/Stock Market; (b) ©Jim McDonald/Corbis; 116 ©Wayne Aldridge/International Stock; 118-119 ©PhotoDisc, Inc.; 122 ©Corbis; 124, 126 ©Arthur Morris/The Stock Market; 128 ©Corbis; 130 (t) ©PhotoDisc, Inc.; (b) ©Archivo Iconografico, S.A./Corbis; 132 ©PhotoDisc, Inc.; 134 ©Jeff Foott/Bruce Coleman, Inc./PictureQuest; 136 ©Sygma/Corbis; 137 ©Bruce Hands/Stock Boston, Inc./PictureQuest; 138 (t) ©Sygma/Corbis; (b) ©Corbis; 140 ©PhotoDisc, Inc.; 141 ©O'Brien Productions/Corbis; 143 ©PhotoDisc, Inc.; 144 ©Craig Tuttle/The Stock Market; 146 (t) ©CMCD/PhotoDisc, Inc.; middle (m) ©Corbis; (b) ©C Squared Studios/PhotoDisc, Inc.; 147 ©Corbis; 148 ©C Squared Studios/PhotoDisc, Inc.; 150 ©Corbis; 151 ©PhotoDisc, Inc.; 152 (l) ©Bettmann/Corbis; (r) ©PhotoDisc, Inc.; 153, 154 ©Bettmann/Corbis; 156 ©PhotoDisc, Inc.; 157 (bowl) ©Comstock, Inc.; (kernels) ©MetaTools; 160 ©EyeWire, Inc.; 162 ©PhotoDisc, Inc.; 163 ©Corbis; 166 ©Quarasan; 168 ©PhotoDisc, Inc.; 172 (fork) ©MetaTools; (rag) ©PhotoDisc, Inc.; 174 (t) ©Quarto Inc./Artville; (b) ©MetaTools; 175-177 ©PhotoDisc, Inc.; 178 ©Joanna B. Pinneo/Aurora/PictureQuest; 180 (t) ©Jonathan Blair/Corbis; (b) ©VCL/FPG International; 180-181 (peanut) ©Comstock, Inc.; 181 (t) ©Corbis; (b) ©Chip Simons/FPG International; 182 ©Corbis; 184 ©Peter Langone/International Stock; 185, 188 ©Joe Atlas/Artville; 190 ©PhotoDisc, Inc.; 191 ©Corbis; 196 ©Quarasan; 199 ©SuperStock, Inc.; 200 ©PhotoDisc, Inc.; 202 ©Courtesy NASA; 206 ©Corbis; 207 ©PhotoDisc, Inc.; 209 (t) ©Digital Studios; (b) ©Roger Ressmeyer/Corbis; 210 ©Courtesy NASA; 211 ©Corbis. Dictionary photos: 214 ©David Woods/The Stock Market; 224 ©Gunter Marx/Corbis; 227 ©Leonard Lee Rue III/Photo Researchers. Additional dictionary photos by: Comstock Klips, Corbis, PhotoDisc, Steck-Vaughn Collection.

ART CREDITS

Roger Chandler 145, 197, 206; David Austin Clar 9, 43, 139; Doug Cushman 27, 106 (t); Michael DiGiorgio 204, 205, 208; Karen Dugan 49, 73 (b); Peter Fasolino 39, 55, 111, 183; Ruth Flanigan 97, 98, 140; Robert Frank 186-188; Susan Guevara 33, 77, 89; Laurie Hamilton 5, 15, 38 (b), 158-160, 174, 179; Laura Jacobsen 164-166; John Kanzler 38 (t); Cheryl Kirk-Noll 119, 120, 170-172; Brian Lies 22-24, 106 (b), 117, 169; John Lund 28-30, 72, 83, 85, 86, 123; Erin Mauterer 50-52; Kathleen O'Malley 10-12, 135, 175, 200; Kevin O'Malley 65, 102-104; Daniel Powers 4, 61, 73 (t), 90-92; Ilene Robinette 3, 68-70; Stacey Schuett 78-80, 93, 189, 203; Jeff Shelly 115, 129; Jason Wolff 107, 125; Marshall Woksa 192-194.

Softcover ISBN 0-7398-3612-9   Hardcover ISBN 0-7398-5056-3

The words *banana, bridge, grass, leaf,* and *monkey* are hidden on the cover. Can you find them?

Contents

Unit 1

Unit 2

Unit 3

Unit 4

Unit 5

Unit 6

Study Steps to Learn a Word

(1) **Say** the word. What consonant sounds do you hear? What vowel sounds do you hear? How many syllables do you hear?

(2) **Look** at the letters in the word. Think about how each sound is spelled. Find any spelling patterns or parts that you know. Close your eyes. Picture the word in your mind.

(3) **Spell** the word aloud.

(4) **Write** the word. Say each letter as you write it.

(5) **Check** the spelling. If you did not spell the word correctly, use the study steps again.

Use the steps on this page to study words that are hard for you.

Spelling Strategies

What can you do when you aren't sure how to spell a word?

Say the word aloud. Make sure you say it correctly. Listen to the sounds in the word. Think about letters and patterns that might spell the sounds.

Look in the Spelling Table to find common spellings for sounds in the word.

Think about related words. They may help you spell the word you're not sure of.

discover—cover

Guess the spelling of the word and check it in a dictionary.

Write the word in different ways. Compare the spellings and choose the one that looks correct.

trale (trail) treighl treal

Think about any spelling rules you know that can help you spell the word.

When a singular word ends in s, ch, sh, or x, -es is added to form the plural.

Listen for a common word part, such as a prefix, suffix, or ending.

careful   beginning

Break the word into syllables and think about how each syllable might be spelled.

Sat ur day
sur prise

Create a memory clue to help you remember the spelling of the word.

I hear with my ear.

Lesson 1
Words with Short *a*

stamp

1. *a* Words

_____
_____
_____
_____
_____
_____
_____
_____
_____
_____
_____
_____
_____
_____
_____
_____
_____
_____

2. *au* Words

_____
_____
_____

past
match
ask
snack
stamp
magic
pass
laugh
happen
answer
travel
plastic
grass
aunt
began
crack
glad
branch
half
banana

Say and Listen

Say each spelling word. Listen for the short *a* sound.

Think and Sort

Look at the letters in each word. Think about how short *a* is spelled. Spell each word aloud.

Short *a* can be shown as /ă/. How many spelling patterns for /ă/ do you see?

1. Write the **eighteen** spelling words that have the *a* pattern.

2. Write the **two** spelling words that have the *au* pattern.

Use the steps on page 6 to study words that are hard for you.

Spelling Patterns

a	au
glad	laugh

Spelling and Meaning

Definitions   Write the spelling word for each definition.
Use the Spelling Dictionary if you need to.

1. a sharp snapping sound _____
2. to come to pass _____
3. special effects and tricks _____
4. to go from place to place _____
5. to set a foot down loudly _____
6. green plants that people mow _____
7. a substance made from chemicals _____

Analogies   An analogy states that two words go together in the same way as two others. Write the spelling word that completes each analogy.

8. *Opened* is to *closed* as _____ is to *ended*.
9. *Bad* is to *good* as *sad* is to _____.
10. *Three* is to *six* as _____ is to *whole*.
11. *Spin* is to *twirl* as *reply* is to _____.
12. *Large* is to *small* as *feast* is to _____.
13. *Vegetable* is to *spinach* as *fruit* is to _____.
14. *Arm* is to *body* as _____ is to *tree*.
15. *Black* is to *white* as *cry* is to _____.
16. *Male* is to *female* as *uncle* is to _____.
17. *Tomorrow* is to *yesterday* as *future* is to _____.
18. *Question* is to _____ as *tell* is to *answer*.
19. *New* is to *old* as *fail* is to _____.

Word Story   Homographs are words that are spelled alike but have different meanings. One spelling word is a homograph that comes from *macche*, meaning "a husband and wife." It also comes from *meiche*, meaning "candle wick." Write the spelling word.

20. _____

Family Tree: pass   Think about how the *pass* words are alike in spelling and meaning. Then add another *pass* word to the tree.

passage

bypass

21.

passed

passable

pass

A Summer Storm

Adam followed his sister down the path from their aunt's cabin. Molly was hurrying to the lake.

"What's taking you so long?" Molly turned to _____ Adam.

1

"I'm *trying* to catch up," was Adam's _____. He was carrying a

2

bag of apples, a _____, and a big _____ cooler.

3   4

"I stopped to get a _____ for us to eat."

5

"We won't have any time to explore the island if we don't hurry," Molly pointed

out. "It's already _____ three."

6

They pushed their canoe into the water. As Molly _____ to

7

paddle, Adam ate an apple. He looked up at the sky. "I don't like the way the

clouds look," he said.

"Oh, they'll _____," Molly told him. "Come on and help me

8

out. This isn't a _____ canoe! It won't row by itself. I've paddled

9

_____ the distance by myself."

10

Adam reached for a paddle. The canoe tipped dangerously. "Be careful!" Molly told Adam. "I don't want to get wet."

"I don't either," said Adam. He sat still and carefully began to paddle. Soon he was able to _____ the speed Molly
set. The canoe glided across the lake.

Suddenly a loud _____ of thunder exploded above
them. The two looked up at the sky. "I was afraid that this might
_____!" shouted Adam. "We have to get off this lake!"

Molly and Adam stopped paddling, wondering if they should
_____ on to the island or go back to the cabin. "Back
to the cabin!" they shouted at once. Lightning flashed across the sky,
and rain began to fall.

Finally they reached the shore. Through the downpour Adam and
Molly could see their _____ standing on the cabin
porch. She had a worried look on her face. The two children jumped
out of the canoe and headed toward her. "Oh, no!" Adam cried as he
tripped over a broken tree _____ and fell hard onto
the wet green _____. Molly helped him up and they
were on their way again. At last they reached the cabin porch.

Adam and Molly began to _____ their feet and
shake some of the rain off. "Wow! That was close," Molly said.
"I'm _____ we're off that lake!"

Adam nodded and began to _____.
"Me too," he said. "We wouldn't want to get
wet, now would we?"

past
match
ask
snack
stamp
magic
pass
laugh
happen
answer
travel
plastic
grass
aunt
began
crack
glad
branch
half
banana

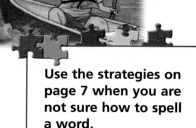

past
match
ask
snack
stamp
magic
pass
laugh
happen
answer
travel
plastic
grass
aunt
began
crack
glad
branch
half
banana

Write to the Point

Have you ever been caught outdoors in a storm like Molly and Adam? Write a brief story about what happened, or use your imagination to make up a story. Tell where you were and what you were doing. Then explain what you did to escape the bad weather. Try to use spelling words from this lesson.

Use the strategies on page 7 when you are not sure how to spell a word.

Proofreading

Proofread the news article below. Use proofreading marks to correct five spelling mistakes, three punctuation mistakes, and two missing words.

Proofreading Marks

◯ spell correctly

⊙ add period

∧ add

Monroe School Monthly

Weather Safety

When you are outside, be aware of the weather.

Watch sky and listen for thunder If you hear loud

crak, find shelter right away. A storm can travl fast.

To be safe, never take shelter under a tree bransh.

If you hapen to be in a boat, head for shore You

will probably be out of danger soon. Most storms

pas quickly

Dictionary Skills

Alphabetical Order   Dictionary words are listed in alphabetical order. Words beginning with *a* come first, then words beginning with *b*, and so on. When the first letter of words is the same, the second letter is used to put the words in alphabetical order. If the first two letters are the same, the third letter is used. Write each group of words in alphabetical order.

1. laugh   glad   stamp

_____   _____   _____

2. plastic   magic   grass

_____   _____   _____

3. began   banana   brick

_____   _____   _____

4. aunt   ask   answer

_____   _____   _____

5. half   have   happy

_____   _____   _____

6. crack   crumb   crisp

_____   _____   _____

Challenge Yourself

What do you think each Challenge Word means? Check the Spelling Dictionary to see if you are right. Then use separate paper to write sentences showing that you understand the meaning of each Challenge Word.

Challenge Words	
acrobat	axle
absence	tragic

7. The **absence** of clouds made us forget that a storm was coming.

8. The road was very bumpy. We thought the wheels on our car would fall off the **axle**.

9. The newspaper reported the **tragic** story of three people lost at sea.

10. The wind made the leaf leap and tumble like a circus **acrobat**.

Lesson 2

Words with Long *a*

chase

1. a-consonant-e Words

_____
_____
_____
_____
_____
_____
_____
_____
_____
_____

2. ai Words

_____
_____
_____
_____
_____
_____

3. eigh Words

_____
_____
_____

4. ea Word

_____

awake
chase
paid
eight
mistake
plain
trade
weight
waste
afraid
neighbor
taste
trail
plane
wait
waist
space
break
state
shape

Say and Listen

Say each spelling word. Listen for the long *a* sound.

Think and Sort

Look at the letters in each word. Think about how long *a* is spelled. Spell each word aloud.

Long *a* can be shown as /ā/. How many spelling patterns for /ā/ do you see?

1. Write the **ten** spelling words that have the *a*-consonant-*e* pattern.

2. Write the **six** spelling words that have the *ai* pattern.

3. Look at the word *eight*. The spelling pattern for this word is *eigh*. The *g* and *h* are silent. Write the **three** spelling words that have the *eigh* pattern.

4. Write the **one** spelling word that has the *ea* pattern.

> Use the steps on page 6 to study words that are hard for you.

Spelling Patterns

a-consonant-e plane	ai paid	eigh eight	ea break

Spelling and Meaning

Homophones   Homophones are words that sound alike but have different spellings and meanings. Complete each sentence with the correct homophone.

1. The present without a ribbon looked very _____.

2. I would rather take a train than a _____.

3. Don't _____ your time looking for the note.

4. Wear the belt around your _____.

5. Alex checked his _____ on the scale.

6. Would you please _____ for me after school?

Rhymes   Write the spelling word that completes each sentence and rhymes with the underlined word.

7. I like the _____ of tomato <u>paste</u>.

8. Did the dog _____ the <u>lace</u> ribbon?

9. The boys will _____ the cars they <u>made</u>.

10. Rosa carried a <u>pail</u> down the _____.

11. On what <u>date</u> did Florida become a _____?

12. Draw a <u>face</u> in the empty _____.

13. Ms. <u>Cade</u> _____ for everyone's lunch.

14. What is the _____ of a roll of <u>tape</u>?

15. We have _____ pieces of <u>bait</u> left.

16. Are you ready to <u>take</u> a _____ from your work?

17. It was a _____ to keep the baby <u>awake</u>.

18. He was _____ that he had left the bill <u>unpaid</u>.

19. I want to be _____ when it's time to eat the <u>steak</u>.

Word Story   The Old English word *neahgebur* was made of *neah*, which meant "near," and *gebur*, which meant "dweller." A *neahgebur* was a near dweller. Today the word has the same meaning. Write the word.

20. _____

Family Tree: *break*   Think about how the *break* words are alike in spelling and meaning. Then add another *break* word to the tree.

unbreakable

rebreak

breakfast

21. _____

break

breaks

Use each spelling word once to complete the selection.

Safe Places in the Wild

How would you like to have a coyote for a next-door _____? Would you be
1
_____? When cities grow, people build homes and highways.
2
People and wild animals get closer together. It is _____ that
3
people and wild animals living near one another can lead to problems. The
animals do not have _____ to run and hunt. Because letting
4
animals lose their homes would be a big _____, people make
5
safe places for wild animals. These places are called wildlife refuges.

Many countries, including Canada, Australia, and South Africa, have set aside
wildlife refuges. If you live in the United States, your _____ also
6
has one. Special workers are _____ to take care of a refuge. At a
7
large refuge, workers sometimes fly over the area in a _____.
8
From the air, they check for problems such as flooding or fire. Most refuge
workers love their job. They would not _____ it for any
9
other kind.

Visitors do not have to _____ long to see

10

wildlife at a refuge. Picture yourself at a woodland refuge. As

you follow a _____ along a creek, seven or

11

_____ deer run past. You see a hungry squirrel

12

_____ open a nut for a snack. You watch a coyote

13

_____ a mouse through the grass. The mouse

14

does not _____ any time scurrying into a hole!

15

Birds sing and dart from branch to branch.

Even at night, the woodland animals are busy. All the raccoons

are _____ and looking for food. They enjoy the

16

sweet _____ of wild berries. What is that strange,

17

dark _____ in a tree? It is an owl watching for

18

prey. A mother opossum slowly waddles past. She carries a lot of

_____ because her babies ride by clinging to her

19

back. She looks as if she has a belt of babies wrapped around her

_____!

20

Wildlife refuges are special places. The animals have a safe place

to live. People can enjoy them, too. Visitors can take a close look

at animals in the wild.

Word list (spiral notebook):

awake
chase
paid
eight
mistake
plain
trade
weight
waste
afraid
neighbor
taste
trail
plane
wait
waist
space
break
state
shape

awake
chase
paid
eight
mistake
plain
trade
weight
waste
afraid
neighbor
taste
trail
plane
wait
waist
space
break
state
shape

Write to the Point

Suppose you are planning a visit to a wildlife refuge. Is there a favorite animal that you would like to see? Write a paragraph telling about the animal. Explain why you would like to see it. Try to use spelling words from this lesson.

> Use the strategies on page 7 when you are not sure how to spell a word.

Proofreading

Proofread the advertisement below. Use proofreading marks to correct five spelling mistakes, three capitalization mistakes, and two unnecessary words.

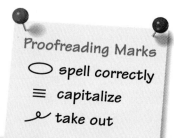

Proofreading Marks
◯ spell correctly
≡ capitalize
✐ take out

Visit Big Mountain Park

are you planning a visit to our stait?

Be sure to to stop at Big Mountain Park.

Climb the trale to Crystal Falls. Taiste the

clean mountain water. see bears and deer

along the way. Enjoy the wide open spase.

it would be be a misstake to miss this

great place!

For park information, call (800) 652-0093.

Using the Spelling Table

How can you find a word in a dictionary when you are not sure how to spell it? A spelling table can help you find the word. Suppose you are not sure how the long *a* sound in *neighbor* is spelled. You can use a spelling table to find the different spellings for long *a*. First, find the pronunciation symbol for long *a*. Then read the first spelling listed for /ā/, and look up *na* words in the dictionary. Look for each spelling until you find *neighbor*.

Sound	Spellings	Examples
/ā/	a a_e ai ay ea eigh ey	April, chase, plain, day, break, eight, obey

Write each of the following words, spelling the long *a* sound in dark type correctly. Use the Spelling Table entry for /ā/ given above and the Spelling Dictionary.

1. chas _____

2. awak _____

3. trad _____

4. ralroad _____

5. rotat _____

6. shap _____

7. tral _____

8. lightwat _____

9. acquant _____

10. betra _____

11. sav _____

Challenge Yourself

Use the Spelling Dictionary to answer these questions. Then use separate paper to write sentences showing that you understand the meaning of each Challenge Word.

Challenge Words	
acquaint	betray
lightweight	reign

12. Can you **acquaint** yourself with people by talking to them for a while? _____

13. Would good citizens **betray** their country by selling its secrets to an enemy? _____

14. Do dark clouds often come before a **reign**? _____

15. In summer do most people wear **lightweight** clothing? _____

Lesson 3

Words with Short *e*

bread

1. *e* Words

_____
_____
_____
_____
_____
_____
_____
_____
_____

2. *ea* Words

_____
_____
_____
_____
_____
_____
_____

3. *ai* Words

_____
_____

4. *ie* Word

_____

5. *ue* Word

_____

again
edge
bread
ever
ready
never
echo
energy
heavy
friend
health
guess
breakfast
fence
stretch
weather
yesterday
desert
sweater
against

Say and Listen

Say each spelling word. Listen for the short e sound.

Think and Sort

Look at the letters in each word. Think about how short e is spelled. Spell each word aloud.

Short e can be shown as /ĕ/. How many spelling patterns for /ĕ/ do you see?

1. Write the **nine** spelling words that have the *e* pattern.

2. Write the **seven** spelling words that have the *ea* pattern.

3. Write the **two** spelling words that have the *ai* pattern.

4. Write the **one** spelling word that has the *ie* pattern.

5. Write the **one** spelling word that has the *ue* pattern.

Use the steps on page 6 to study words that are hard for you.

Spelling Patterns

e	ea	ai	ie	ue
fence	**ready**	**again**	**friend**	**guess**

Spelling and Meaning

Antonyms   Antonyms are words that have opposite meanings. Write the spelling word that is an antonym of each word.

1. swamp _____
2. sickness _____
3. enemy _____
4. know _____
5. lightweight _____
6. always _____
7. center _____
8. for _____
9. tomorrow _____
10. unprepared _____

Common Phrases   Write the spelling word that completes each phrase.

11. again and _____
12. happily _____ after
13. snowy _____
14. _____ and butter
15. skirt and _____
16. jump over the _____
17. bend and _____
18. the _____ of your voice
19. _____ from the sun

Word Story   Have you ever fasted? To fast is to go a long time without eating. We all fast when we sleep at night. Our first meal of the day breaks, or ends, our fast. Write the spelling word that names this meal.

20. _____

Family Tree: *friend*   Think about how the *friend* words are alike in spelling and meaning. Then add another *friend* word to the tree.

friendlier

friendliness

friendliest

21.

friends

friend   unfriendly

Use each spelling word once to complete the story.

Seymour Finds a Friend

The autumn _____ was just right for tennis. Seymour C. Skunk
                              1

put on his white tennis _____ and shorts. He ran to the court,
                              2

feeling full of _____. He knew that playing tennis was good for his
                3

_____. Tennis helped him strengthen and _____
                4   5

his muscles.

"If only I had someone to play with," Seymour sighed. "All the other animals

always turn up their nose at me. They whisper 'P-U' under their breath. I would

_____ treat someone that way."
                6

Seymour listened to the _____ of his own voice. He felt as though
                              7

he were all alone on a _____ island. With a _____
                        8   9

heart, Seymour gave the ball a smack _____ a wall.
                                        10

"Great form!" said a young rabbit as she hopped over the _____
                                                          11

around the court.

"How about a game?" he asked.

The rabbit smiled. She followed him to the tennis court. After the game,

Seymour invited the pretty rabbit to have some _____.
                                                12

"Are you _____ to order?" asked the waiter. He was holding
            13

his nose.

"I will have the forty-carrot muffins," said the rabbit.

"I'll try the spinach surprise. And please bring some French

_____," said Seymour. He glanced at the rabbit.
         14

"What's your name?" he asked.

The rabbit covered her nose with her paws. She gave Seymour

quite a start.

"I'm Beatrice Lapin," she answered in a soft voice. "But everyone

calls me Bunny."

"You know, Bunny," said Seymour slowly, "_____
                                              15

my life was sad. I didn't think I'd _____ find a
                                        16

_____ like you."
         17

Bunny covered her nose _____.
                               18

Seymour jumped to the _____ of his seat.
                             19

"There's something I must ask you," he began. "It's a rather

'scent-sitive' subject."

"I know," said Bunny sadly. "You couldn't help but notice that

my nose is extremely large."

"Why, Bunny," Seymour said, "I never even noticed your nose.

I've been busy thinking my

smell was bothering you."

"Why, Seymour, I hadn't

even noticed your smell,"

Bunny smiled and said.

"I _____
        20

both of us were busy

worrying about ourselves!"

again
edge
bread
ever
ready
never
echo
energy
heavy
friend
health
guess
breakfast
fence
stretch
weather
yesterday
desert
sweater
against

again
edge
bread
ever
ready
never
echo
energy
heavy
friend
health
guess
breakfast
fence
stretch
weather
yesterday
desert
sweater
against

Write to the Point

Seymour C. Skunk was unhappy until he found a friend. Write a paragraph about a person who is your friend. Tell why you like having the person as a friend. Try to use spelling words from this lesson.

Use the strategies on page 7 when you are not sure how to spell a word.

Proofreading

Proofread the journal entry below. Use proofreading marks to correct five spelling mistakes, three capitalization mistakes, and two missing words.

Proofreading Marks

⬭ spell correctly

≡ capitalize

∧ add

july 21

    Yestarday morning I played tennis my frend Maria. The wether was hot, and we had not eaten much brekfast. we didn't have very much enerjy. I could hardly hit the ball. maria couldn't run very far or very fast.

    We will not make the same mistake again. Next time we'll start day with a bigger meal.

Dictionary Skills

Guide Words Guide words are the two words in dark type at the top of each dictionary page. The first guide word is the first entry word on the page. The second guide word is the last entry word. The other entry words on the page are arranged in alphabetical order between the guide words. When searching for a word in a dictionary, use the guide words to find the correct page.

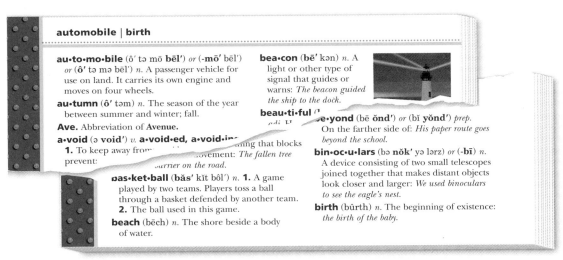

automobile | birth

au·to·mo·bile (ô′ tə mō bēl′) *or* (-mō′ bēl′) *or* (ô′ tə mə bēl′) *n.* A passenger vehicle for use on land. It carries its own engine and moves on four wheels.

au·tumn (ô′ təm) *n.* The season of the year between summer and winter; fall.

Ave. Abbreviation of **Avenue.**

a·void (ə void′) *v.* **a·void·ed, a·void·in-**
1. To keep away fro~~m~~ ~~...~~ ~~...~~ing that blocks
prevent: ~~...~~ ~~...~~vement: *The fallen tree*
~~...~~urrier on the road.

bas·ket·ball (băs′ kĭt bôl′) *n.* **1.** A game played by two teams. Players toss a ball through a basket defended by another team. **2.** The ball used in this game.

beach (bēch) *n.* The shore beside a body of water.

bea·con (bē′ kən) *n.* A light or other type of signal that guides or warns: *The beacon guided the ship to the dock.*

beau·ti·ful ~~(...~~ ~~...~~ ~~...~~

be·yond (bē ŏnd′) *or* (bĭ yŏnd′) *prep.* On the farther side of: *His paper route goes beyond the school.*

bin·oc·u·lars (bə nŏk′ yə lərz) *or* (-bī) *n.* A device consisting of two small telescopes joined together that makes distant objects look closer and larger: *We used binoculars to see the eagle's nest.*

birth (bûrth) *n.* The beginning of existence: *the birth of the baby.*

Each pair of guide words below is followed by a list of words. Write the list words that are on the same dictionary page as the guide words.

1. after/agree   ace   again   age   afraid

_____   _____

2. straight/sweet   stamp   sweater   stretch   switch

_____   _____

3. head/height   health   help   hamster   heavy

_____   _____

Challenge Yourself

Write the Challenge Word for each clue. Check the Spelling Dictionary to see if you are right. Then use separate paper to write sentences showing that you understand the meaning of each Challenge Word.

Challenge Words

kennel   sheriff
cleanse   deafen

4. You should always do this to a cut or scrape before you put on a bandage. _____

5. This person's job is to make sure laws are kept. _____

6. A very loud sound near your ear could do this to you. _____

7. You might say this place has gone to the dogs! _____

Lesson 4

Words with Long *e*

beach

1. *ea* Words

_____
_____
_____
_____
_____
_____
_____
_____
_____
_____
_____

2. *ee* Words

_____
_____
_____
_____
_____
_____
_____
_____
_____

season
knee
queen
scream
reason
between
sweep
sweet
speech
beach
seem
teach
means
speak
freeze
leaf
treat
squeeze
peace
please

Say and Listen

Say each spelling word. Listen for the long e sound.

Think and Sort

Look at the letters in each word. Think about how long e is spelled. Spell each word aloud.

Long e can be shown as /ē/. How many spelling patterns for /ē/ do you see?

1. Write the **eleven** spelling words that have the *ea* pattern.

2. Write the **nine** spelling words that have the *ee* pattern.

Use the steps on page 6 to study words that are hard for you.

Spelling Patterns

ea	ee
beach	sweep

Spelling and Meaning

Classifying Write the spelling word that belongs in each group.

1. dust, vacuum, _____
2. king, princess, _____
3. trunk, branch, _____
4. ankle, thigh, _____
5. shout, yell, _____
6. among, beside, _____
7. sour, salty, _____
8. shows, intends, _____

What's the Answer? Write the spelling word that answers each question.

9. What word do you use to politely ask for something? _____
10. What word names a part of the year? _____
11. What do you give a good dog? _____
12. What word means the same as *talk*? _____
13. What word means "appear to be"? _____
14. What do you call a public talk? _____
15. Where do people go to have fun in the summer sun? _____
16. What do you do to get juice from an orange? _____
17. What tells why something happens? _____
18. If a lake gets cold, what might it do? _____
19. What word means the opposite of *war*? _____

Word Story One spelling word was once spelled *taecan*. Later this spelling was changed to *teachen*. The word means "to instruct or to guide in education." Write the spelling we use today.

20. _____

Family Tree: *sweet* Think about how the *sweet* words are alike in spelling and meaning. Then add another *sweet* word to the tree.

sweetly

sweeten

21. _____

sweetener

sweet

sweeter

Use each spelling word once to complete the story.

The Big Race

It was the day of the big race. The track team was having its last meet

of the _____1_____. Ella stood with the other runners, waiting for

her event. It was the last race of the day.

"I'm scared," she said to her friend Rachel. "Look at me. I'm shaking

like a _____2_____."

"You're scared?" Rachel squeaked. "I'm so nervous I can hardly

_____3_____."

"Really? You always _____4_____ so calm," Ella answered.

Coach Talbot knelt on one _____5_____ and gave his same old

_____6_____ to Ella. "I'll make this short and _____7_____,"

he said. "The one thing I've tried to _____8_____ you is that

it's how you play the game that counts. Just because this final race

_____9_____ winning the district championship, that's no

_____10_____ for you to be scared."

Rachel gave Ella's hand a _____11_____ and she whispered,

"You can do it!"

Ella took her place at the starting line. Suddenly she felt weak. She

was afraid that she would _____12_____ up at the starting whistle.

She closed her eyes and imagined that she was running along the sandy

_____13_____ again. She tried to remember the _____14_____

and quiet of those early mornings.

"Starting places, _____15_____," the judge began. "On your mark,

get set, . . ." He blew the whistle, and the runners were on their way!

Ella got off to a slow start. As she struggled to speed up, she heard the rest of her team _____ "Go, Ella, Go!" Ella's legs began to move steadily faster.

As she rounded the last turn, Ella was ahead of all but three runners. It was time to make her move. With only a few yards left, Ella passed _____ two of the runners in front of her. The crowd began to roar. Ella felt as though she were flying! Soon the front runner began to drop back. She had used up all her energy at the beginning of the race. Ella felt herself _____ past the tired runner and break the tape. Her team had won!

Coach Talbot jumped for joy and shook Ella's hand. "Fantastic race!" he said to her. Then he looked at the team and said, "Girls, you've earned a _____. I'll take you out for ice cream. You can each have a _____-size cone!"

"Thanks, coach. You're a sport!" the girls said happily and piled into his car.

season
knee
queen
scream
reason
between
sweep
sweet
speech
beach
seem
teach
means
speak
freeze
leaf
treat
squeeze
peace
please

Spelling and Writing

season
knee
queen
scream
reason
between
sweep
sweet
speech
beach
seem
teach
means
speak
freeze
leaf
treat
squeeze
peace
please

Write to the Point

"The Big Race" is about running. What is your favorite sport? Write a paragraph about it. Tell what makes that sport exciting to play or watch. Try to use spelling words from this lesson.

Use the strategies on page 7 when you are not sure how to spell a word.

Proofreading

Proofread the e-mail message below. Use proofreading marks to correct five spelling mistakes, three punctuation mistakes, and two missing words.

Proofreading Marks
◯ spell correctly
? add question mark
∧ add

---

e-mail

| Address Book | Attachment | Check Spelling | Send | Save Draft | Cancel |

Dear Jan,

Have you ever been a member a track team Running can really teech you what hard work meens. We run every seasen of year. It seems as if I either freaze or melt. Some days it doesn't seem worth it. Then we win, and I remember the reeson that I joined the team.

What have you been doing this spring Are you playing tennis again Let me know when you can come for a visit.

Chang

Language Connection

Verbs   A verb is a word that expresses action or being.

> I **ran** across the street.   Ling **is** a good writer.

Write the verb in each group of words.

1. sweep   girl   swan

   _____

2. leaf   neat   seem

   _____

3. team   scream   queen

   _____

4. between   sweet   means

   _____

5. speak   peace   plain

   _____

6. cheese   squeeze   knee

   _____

⭐ Challenge Yourself

Write the Challenge Word for each clue. Check the Spelling Dictionary to see if you are right. Then use separate paper to write sentences showing that you understand the meaning of each Challenge Word.

Challenge Words	
beacon	conceal
treason	meek

7. When you hide something, you do this to it.   _____

8. Someone who is quiet and gentle is this.   _____

9. If you help your country's enemies, you are guilty of this crime.

   _____

10. The light at the top of a lighthouse is this.   _____

Months, Days, and Titles

April

Say and Listen

Say the spelling words. Listen to the sounds in each word.

Think and Sort

Look at the letters in each word. Spell each word aloud.

An **abbreviation** is a shortened form of a word. *Mr.* is an abbreviation for *Mister.*

A **syllable** is a word part with one vowel sound. *Sun* has one syllable. *Sunny* has two syllables.

1. Write the **one** spelling word that is the abbreviation of *Doctor.*
2. Write the **three** spelling words that have one syllable.
3. Write the **nine** spelling words that have two syllables.
4. Write the **five** spelling words that have three syllables.
5. Write the **two** spelling words that have four syllables.

October
February
Friday
March
Thursday
December
July
May
Dr.
August
Sunday
June
Monday
September
Tuesday
January
November
Saturday
Wednesday
April

1. Abbreviation
2. One-Syllable Words
3. Two-Syllable Words
4. Three-Syllable Words
5. Four-Syllable Words

Use the steps on page 6 to study words that are hard for you.

Spelling Patterns

One Syllable	Two Syllables	Three Syllables	Four Syllables
March	A•pril	Sep•tem•ber	Jan•u•ar•y

Spelling and Meaning

Clues   Write the spelling word for each clue.

1. the month to send valentines _____
2. the first day of the week _____
3. the day after Monday _____
4. the last month of the year _____
5. the first month of autumn _____
6. the first day of the weekend _____
7. the month before December _____
8. the day in the middle of the week _____
9. the month after March _____
10. the first day of the school week _____
11. the month after September _____
12. the day before Friday _____
13. the month between July and September _____
14. a short way to write *Doctor* _____

Rhymes   Write the spelling word that completes each sentence and rhymes with the underlined word or words.

15. We can <u>play</u> outside in _____.
16. Will the month of _____ be here <u>soon</u>?
17. Kwan visited the Gateway <u>Arch</u> in _____.
18. I gave Dad a new <u>tie</u> in _____.
19. The new <u>highway</u> will be open on _____.

Word Story   Janus was the Roman god of beginnings and endings. He had two faces so that he could see both things. The Romans named the first month after Janus. Write the spelling word that comes from *Janus*.

20. _____

Family Tree: *Sunday*   *Sunday* comes from the word *sun*. Think about how the *sun* words are alike in spelling and meaning. Then add another *sun* word to the tree.

sunny

Sunday

suntan

sunning

21. _____

sun

The Stories Behind the Names

Have you ever wondered how the days of our week and the months of our year got their names? The first two days of the week were named by people in England hundreds of years ago. They named the first day

_____ to honor the sun. They called the second day Moon's
1

Day, or _____, to honor the moon.
2

The names of the next four days of our week come from ancient Norway. Norwegians named one day Tyr's Day to honor their god, Tyr. Tyr's Day

later became known as _____.
3

Tyr's father was the god Woden. His day was called Woden's Day, which

we now call _____. Woden had a wife named Frigg. The
4

Norwegians named one day of the week after her. They called it Frigg's Day,

or _____.
5

Thor

The most powerful Norse god was Thor, the god of

thunder. We call Thor's Day _____.
6

The last day of the week, _____, is
7

named for Saturn, the ancient Roman god of planting.

The names of our months also come from the

ancient Romans, who spoke Latin. The month of

_____ is named for the Roman god
8

Janus. Janus had two faces. One face looked into

the past. The other looked into the new year. The

January February March April May June Ju

name of the second month,

_____, comes from
9

the Latin word *februa*, which meant

"pure." The name of the next month,

_____, comes from Mars,
10

the Roman war god. The Latin word

for *open* was *aprilis*. From *aprilis*

comes _____, the
11

month when flowers open. Maia was

the goddess of spring. The month of

_____ is named for her.
12

The month of _____ is named
13

for the goddess Juno.

Augustus Caesar

October
February
Friday
March
Thursday
December
July
May
Dr.
August
Sunday
June
Monday
September
Tuesday
January
November
Saturday
Wednesday
April

The names of two months come from the names of Roman

emperors. _____ is named for Julius Caesar.
14

_____ is named for Augustus, his nephew.
15

The last four months come from Latin words for the

numbers seven through ten: *septem, octo, novem, decem*. The

Roman year started in March, so the seventh month was

_____. The eighth was _____.
16   17

The ninth was _____, and the tenth was _____.
18   19

We know the history of names because some people have spent years

studying words and where they came from. One of these people is

_____ Wilfred Funk. Dr. Funk wrote, "Words truly are little
20

windows through which we can look into the past." We are grateful to Dr.

Funk and people like him for sharing what they see.

October
February
Friday
March
Thursday
December
July
May
Dr.
August
Sunday
June
Monday
September
Tuesday
January
November
Saturday
Wednesday
April

Write to the Point

Which month do you like best? Write a paragraph that tells your favorite month and the reasons why you like it. Try to use spelling words from this lesson.

Use the strategies on page 7 when you are not sure how to spell a word.

Proofreading

Proofread the list below. Use proofreading marks to correct five spelling mistakes, three capitalization mistakes, and two unnecessary words.

Proofreading Marks
○ spell correctly
≡ capitalize
℘ take out

Things to Do

1. call Dtr. wilson on Munday

2. bring newspapers to class on Toosday

3. go to to hockey practice on Thursday

4. turn in science report on Frieday

5. sweep driveway and take out trash on saturday

6. get present for eric's birthday party on Febuary 15

7. sign up for the the class trip in April

Dictionary Skills

Syllables A syllable is a word or word part that has one vowel sound. If an entry word in the Spelling Dictionary has more than one syllable, dots are used to separate the syllables.

June has one syllable.

> **June** (jōōn) *n.* The sixth month of the year.

October has three syllables.

> **Oc·to·ber** (ŏk tō′ bər) *n.* The tenth month of the year.

Rewrite each word, using dots or lines to divide it into syllables. Use the Spelling Dictionary if you need help

1. January   _____
2. February   _____
3. April   _____
4. July   _____
5. August   _____
6. September   _____
7. November   _____
8. December   _____
9. Monday   _____
10. Wednesday   _____
11. Thursday   _____
12. Friday   _____
13. Saturday   _____

Challenge Yourself

Use the Spelling Dictionary to answer these questions. Then use separate paper to write sentences showing that you understand the meaning of each Challenge Word.

Challenge Words	
Ms.	Pres.
Gov.	Jr.

14. Is **Ms.** Pat Brown a woman? _____

15. Does the title *Pres.* before a person's name mean that the person is present? _____

16. What kind of job does **Gov.** Sanchez have? _____

17. Is Jeffrey Smith, **Jr.**, named after his father? _____

Lesson 6

Unit 1 Review
Lessons 1–5

Use the steps on page 6 to study words that are hard for you.

 1

travel
answer
half
laugh
aunt

Words With Short *a*

Write the spelling word that completes each sentence.

1. I know the _____ to that question.
2. My dog likes to _____ in our van.
3. My mother's sister is my _____.
4. I saved _____ of my sandwich for later.
5. Grandpa's funny stories make me _____.

 2

mistake
taste
afraid
eight
neighbor
break

Words with Long *a*

Write the spelling word for each definition. Use the Spelling Dictionary if you need to.

6. scared _____
7. the number after seven _____
8. a wrong choice _____
9. the sense that recognizes flavor _____
10. someone living nearby _____
11. to split apart _____

 3

energy
stretch
sweater
against
friend
guess

Words with Short *e*

Write the spelling word that belongs in each group.

12. pal, buddy, _____
13. grow, lengthen, _____
14. beside, toward, _____
15. power, strength, _____

16. coat, jacket, _____

17. think, suppose, _____

4 Words with Long e

knee
speech
reason
please

Write the spelling word that completes each analogy.

18. _When_ is to _time_ as _why_ is to _____.

19. _Question_ is to _answer_ as _____ is to _thank you_.

20. _Elbow_ is to _arm_ as _____ is to _leg_.

21. _Notes_ is to _music_ as _words_ is to _____.

5 Months, Days, and Titles

Dr.
Wednesday
February
January

Write the spelling word that answers each question.

22. What is the first month of the new year? _____

23. What is the shortest month? _____

24. What day falls in the middle of the week? _____

25. What is the abbreviation for _Doctor_? _____

26. /ă/ Words

_____

_____

_____

_____

_____

27. /ā/ Words

_____

_____

_____

_____

_____

28. /ĕ/ Words

_____

_____

_____

_____

_____

29. /ē/ Words

_____

_____

_____

_____

_____

Review Sort

half	travel	speech	answer
sweater	laugh	taste	neighbor
please	aunt	eight	knee
energy	stretch	reason	break
mistake	guess	friend	

26. Write the **five** short *a* words. Circle the letters that spell /ă/ in each word.

27. Write the **five** long *a* words. Circle the letters that spell /ā/ in each word.

28. Write the **five** short *e* words. Circle the letters that spell /ĕ/ in each word.

29. Write the **four** long *e* words. Circle the letters that spell /ē/ in each word.

These six words have been sorted into three groups. Explain how the words in each group are alike.

30. **Wednesday**   **April**

_____

_____

31. **Saturday**   **October**

_____

_____

32. **January**   **February**

_____

_____

Writer's Workshop

A Personal Narrative

A personal narrative tells the story of something that happened to you. It also might tell how you felt about what happened. Because the story is about you, your personal narrative will have pronouns such as *I, me, we*, and *my*. Here is part of Jessica's personal narrative about a big mistake she made.

> **My Biggest Mistake**
>
> I'll never forget the horrible mistake I made in my very first T-ball game. I stepped up to the plate and stared at the ball. Then I swung the bat as hard as I could. When I felt it hit the ball, I was so happy! I ran as hard and as fast as I could. On my way to the base, I saw the coach waving his arms. Oh, no! I was running to the wrong base.

Prewriting   To write her personal narrative, Jessica followed the steps in the writing process. After she decided on a topic, she completed a chain of events chart. The chart helped Jessica decide what to include and what to leave out. Part of Jessica's chain of events chart is shown here. Study what she did.

1	2	3
I stepped up to the plate.	I hit the ball really hard.	I ran as fast as I could to the base.

It's Your Turn!

Write your own personal narrative. It can be about your biggest mistake, your greatest moment, or any special event in your life. After you have decided what to write about, make a chain of events chart. Then follow the other steps in the writing process—writing, revising, proofreading, and publishing. Try to use spelling words from this lesson in your personal narrative.

More Words with Long *e*

city

1. *e* Words

_____

_____

2. *y* Words

_____

_____

_____

_____

_____

_____

_____

_____

_____

_____

_____

3. *e*-consonant-*e* Word

_____

4. *eo* Word

_____

5. *i* Words

_____

_____

_____

_____

6. *i*-consonant-*e* Word

_____

people
easy
every
police
radio
zebra
evening
body
family
piano
copy
busy
ski
city
pizza
angry
plenty
hungry
sorry
secret

Say and Listen

Say each spelling word. Listen for the long e sound.

Think and Sort

Look at the letters in each word. Think about how the long e sound is spelled. Spell each word aloud.

Long e can be shown as /ē/. How many spelling patterns for /ē/ do you see?

1. Write the **two** spelling words that have the *e* pattern.

2. Write the **eleven** spelling words that have the *y* pattern.

3. Write the **one** spelling word that has the *e*-consonant-*e* pattern.

4. Write the **one** spelling word that has the *eo* pattern.

5. Write the **four** spelling words that have the *i* pattern.

6. Write the **one** spelling word that has the *i*-consonant-*e* pattern.

Use the steps on page 6 to study words that are hard for you.

Spelling Patterns

e	y	e-consonant-e	eo	i	i-consonant-e
zebra	city	evening	people	ski	police

Spelling and Meaning

Definitions Write the spelling word for each definition.

1. equipment used to receive sounds sent over air waves _____

2. something known only to oneself _____

3. government workers who enforce laws _____

4. feeling sadness or pity _____

5. having a lot to do _____

6. to glide across snow or water _____

7. a pie with cheese and tomato sauce _____

8. a striped animal related to the horse _____

9. to make exactly like another _____

10. a center of people and business _____

11. the entire form of a living thing _____

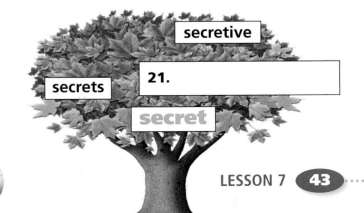

Synonyms Synonyms are words that have the same or almost the same meaning. Write the spelling word that is a synonym for each underlined word.

12. Our homework for tomorrow is <u>simple</u>. _____

13. The teacher gave <u>each</u> student a chore. _____

14. Louis is <u>mad</u> about losing his cap. _____

15. It was a lovely <u>night</u> for a walk. _____

16. Many <u>persons</u> were waiting for the bus. _____

17. We have <u>lots</u> of food for supper. _____

18. Jose's <u>relatives</u> had a reunion last summer. _____

19. I'm <u>starving</u>, so let's eat! _____

Word Story   A musical instrument that can be played both softly and loudly was first made in Italy. The instrument became known by the Italian name *pianoforte*, which means "soft and loud." Soon this name was shortened. Write the spelling word that names the instrument.

20. _____

Family Tree: *secret*   Think about how the *secret* words are alike in spelling and meaning. Then add another *secret* word to the tree.

secretive

secrets

21.

secret

★ ★ Greenville

★ ★ ★ Want Ads ★ ★ ★

Phil Goode Health Club needs teacher for _____- building class. Help out-of-shape _____ exercise and tone their body. Must be able to do push-ups and to jump rope. Must also be able to carry tired customers home. Work hours include four days and one _____ per week. Call I.M. Phitt at 444-5555.

1
2
3

Pop's Parlor needs talented _____ cook who can sing. Must also play the _____ and like preparing mouth-watering food for _____ people. Job requires singing to large crowds. Pop's Parlor is very _____ to reach by bus or train. Call I.E. Talot at 555-4444.

4
5
6
7

Super Sleuth Seeks Support

Too much work! Helper needed for small but _____ spy business. Must be able to keep a _____. I offer you _____ of interesting work. Be prepared to work nights and _____ Saturday and Sunday. Office is near center of _____. Can't tell you where. Send a self-destructing tape to Post Office Box 11 telling why you want the job.

8
9
10
11
12

Gazette ★★

_____ 13 of five with zoo seeks someone to teach good stable manners to pet _____ 14. Must really love lizards, bats, elephants, and other unusual pets. Fax a _____ 15 of a letter from some animal you have taught to 111-2222. Be sure the letter is signed with a clear paw print.

★★★For Sale★★★

Amazing antique AM _____ 16. Ugly frame but works perfectly. Even picks up radio stations from Antarctica, messages to _____ 17 cars, and phone conversations. For more about this special offer, call I.M.N. Eavesdropper at 345-6789.

Skiers: Security and Safety on the Slopes

If you've bought cheap poles, don't get upset or _____ 18 with yourself. Buy our no-spills, no-accident _____ 19 poles. You won't be _____ 20 you bought them. Call us before Friday at 456-7890 and get free book, _Study Guide to Skiing Safety,_ and free pass to any hospital of your choice.

people
easy
every
police
radio
zebra
evening
body
family
piano
copy
busy
ski
city
pizza
angry
plenty
hungry
sorry
secret

For Sale

Write to the Point

Advertising can be a great way to let people know what you want to buy or sell. Write an ad for something you want to buy or sell. Your ad can be silly, like the ones in the lesson, or it can be real. Be sure to give important information as well as interesting details. Try to use spelling words from this lesson.

Use the strategies on page 7 when you are not sure how to spell a word.

Proofreading

Proofread the ad below. Use proofreading marks to correct five spelling mistakes, three capitalization mistakes, and two unnecessary words.

Proofreading Marks
⬭ spell correctly
≡ capitalize
℘ take out

people	
easy	
every	
police	
radio	
zebra	
evening	
body	
family	
piano	
copy	
busy	
ski	
city	
pizza	
angry	
plenty	
hungry	
sorry	
secret	

Yard Sale

Family of seven is having a yard sale! It will be held on saturday, May 7, at 333 Hilly Drive. The house is is eazy to find. Just turn left off Highway 3 at harvey Street. follow the signs at evry street corner. There will be plenty of good stuff and lots of peeple. Come early before we we get too bizzy!

Language Connection

Commas A series is a list of three or more items. Use a comma to separate the items in a series.

> Dave has a cat, a dog, and a hamster.

> On our vacation we rode in a car, flew in a plane, and sailed in a boat.

Write the sentences below, adding commas where they are needed.

1. I told the secret to Amy Will and Edward.

_____

2. I love music so much that I play the violin piano and flute.

_____

3. At the zoo we saw a zebra an elephant and a lion.

_____

4. I like pizza with cheese peppers and onions.

_____

5. Everyone in my family likes to ski skate and sled.

_____

6. The busy city has plenty of people cars and buses.

_____

7. Rita Jenna Karen and Kim play soccer.

_____

Challenge Yourself

What do you think each Challenge Word means? Check the Spelling Dictionary to see if you are right. Then use separate paper to write sentences showing that you understand the meaning of each Challenge Word.

Challenge Words	
attorney	barrier
retrieve	fatigue

8. We asked an **attorney** for advice about the law.

9. The city built a **barrier** to keep snow off the road.

10. Josh has trained his dog to **retrieve** baseballs from the pond.

11. Although I was tired, I didn't let my **fatigue** keep me from my daily jog.

Words with Short *i*

bridge

1. *a* Words

_____

_____

2. *y* Word

_____

3. *i* Words

_____

_____

_____

_____

_____

_____

_____

_____

_____

_____

_____

_____

_____

_____

_____

4. *ui* Words

_____

_____

quick

deliver

gym

different

picture

middle

interesting

village

written

bridge

guitar

thick

picnic

inch

begin

pitch

itch

chicken

building

package

Say and Listen

Say each spelling word. Listen for the short *i* sound.

Think and Sort

Look at the letters in each word. Think about how short *i* is spelled. Spell each word aloud.

Short *i* can be shown as /ĭ/. How many spelling patterns for /ĭ/ do you see?

1. Write the **two** spelling words that have the *a* pattern.

2. Write the **one** spelling word that has the *y* pattern.

3. Write the **fifteen** spelling words that have the *i* pattern.

4. Write the **two** spelling words that have the *ui* pattern.

Use the steps on page 6 to study words that are hard for you.

Spelling Patterns

a	y	i	ui
package	gym	pitch	building

Spelling and Meaning

Antonyms   Write the spelling word that is an antonym of each underlined word.

1. Michael wants to <u>catch</u> the baseball. _____
2. Those two pictures are <u>alike</u>. _____
3. Can we <u>finish</u> reading the story now? _____
4. Yoshi was <u>slow</u> to finish the job. _____
5. The gravy was too <u>thin</u>. _____
6. The movie about whales was very <u>boring</u>. _____
7. I couldn't read the words I had <u>erased</u>. _____
8. The store will <u>receive</u> our new furniture. _____

Classifying   Write the spelling word that belongs in each group.

9. duck, goose, _____
10. foot, yard, _____
11. tunnel, arch, _____
12. beginning, end, _____
13. photo, drawing, _____
14. city, town, _____
15. violin, banjo, _____
16. box, carton, _____
17. tickle, scratch, _____
18. making, constructing, _____
19. cafeteria, classroom, _____

Word Story   The French word *piquenique* once named a gathering of people in which each person brought something to eat. Later the word took on the meaning of "a meal in the open air." Which spelling word names this meal? Write the word.

20. _____

Family Tree: *deliver*   Think about how the *deliver* words are alike in spelling and meaning. Then add another *deliver* word to the tree.

undeliverable   delivers

21. _____

delivering   delivery

deliver

Scrambled Plans

"Don't forget the eggs!" Mom shouted. Alan and Ling climbed aboard the family spaceship. Ling held her baseball and leaned back in her seat.

"Grocery store," Alan told the spaceship's computer, and the spaceship took off. Then Alan saw a light on the control panel _____ 1 to flash. Alan looked at the computer screen. "Ling, we're not headed for the grocery store. The ship has taken a _____ 2 course!"

Two hours later the rocket landed with a bump. Alan and Ling saw that they were in the _____ 3 of some large buildings. Each _____ 4 looked like a giant _____ 5 coop. It was a whole _____ 6 of chicken coops!

As the children climbed out of the ship, a figure flew toward them as _____ 7 as a flash. Alan and Ling saw that it was a giant chicken. It stood an _____ 8 taller than Alan and had a _____ 9 covering of white feathers.

"Welcome, children," he said clearly in English. "We've been EGGS-PECK-ting you! Our great-grandchickens left your planet long ago in search of freedom.

Before they left, they made a _____ record of
10
Earth's most _____ sports. One chicken was in
11
charge of boxing and wrapping the record. When our great-
grandchickens opened the _____, they found that
12
he had left out the directions for playing the game of baseball!"

"And you want us to teach you?" Ling asked.

"EGGS-actly. Once we learn how to play this great game,
we will _____ you safely back to Earth."
13

The children agreed, and the chicken flapped his wings
with delight. "Follow me," the giant chicken told them. The
three crossed over a _____ and walked until
14
they reached a school _____. There Ling and
15
Alan taught the chickens the lost art of baseball. Ling worked
on the _____, and Alan worked on the hit.
16

That evening the chicken planet held its first baseball game.
Everyone brought a _____ supper. Someone
17
played a _____ throughout the game. Soon the
18
score was tied 3 to 3. The pitcher was chewing gum and
scratching an _____ on his beak. A high fly over
19
the head of a left-field chicken ended the game. Alan snapped a
_____ of each team.
20

"Ling, wake up!" a voice said. It was Alan. "We're at the
grocery store. Come on."

"I must have fallen asleep," said Ling. "But I had
the most EGG-citing dream!"

quick
deliver
gym
different
picture
middle
interesting
village
written
bridge
guitar
thick
picnic
inch
begin
pitch
itch
chicken
building
package

Spelling and Writing

quick
deliver
gym
different
picture
middle
interesting
village
written
bridge
guitar
thick
picnic
inch
begin
pitch
itch
chicken
building
package

Write to the Point

Imagine that you have met a creature from another planet. What does the creature look like? How does it sound? How does it move? Write a description of the creature. Try to use spelling words from this lesson.

Use the strategies on page 7 when you are not sure how to spell a word.

Proofreading

Proofread the movie review below. Use proofreading marks to correct five spelling mistakes, three capitalization mistakes, and two punctuation mistakes.

Proofreading Marks
◯ spell correctly
≡ capitalize
? add question mark

Movie Review

A large thik cloud of smoke drops to the earth. The cloud settles on a bridge near a small vilige. It is the middel of the day. people drive their cars over the bridge and through the smoke. Then they disappear! Where do they go Soon the smoke cloud takes the shape of a bilding. firefighters hear voices inside, but no one is quik enough to catch up with it. What is the smoke cloud? Will it return See the movie *Space Visitors* and find out. it's out of this world!

Dictionary Skills

Entry Words   The words listed and explained in a dictionary are called entry words. An entry word in a dictionary is divided into syllables.

> **syl·la·ble** (sĭl′ ə′ bəl) *n*. A single uninterrupted sound forming part of a word or in some cases an entire word.

Read the examples of entry words below. Count how many syllables each word has and write the number.

1. chick•en _____

2. pitch _____

3. de•liv•er _____

Find each of the words below in the Spelling Dictionary. Use dots to write them in syllables.

4. guitar _____

5. picture _____

6. picnic _____

7. written _____

8. begin _____

9. package _____

10. different _____

11. building _____

Challenge Yourself

What do you think each Challenge Word means? Check the Spelling Dictionary to see if you are right. Then use separate paper to write sentences showing that you understand the meaning of each Challenge Word.

Challenge Words
dismal
banish
Gypsy
acknowledge

12. We wanted Saturday to be sunny, but the weather was **dismal**.

13. The king decided to **banish** all thieves to an island.

14. Elisa is a **Gypsy**, but her family doesn't travel from place to place.

15. The captain would not **acknowledge** that they were lost.

Words with Long *i*

lightning

1. *igh* Words

_____
_____
_____
_____
_____
_____
_____
_____
_____
_____
_____
_____
_____

2. *y* Words

_____
_____
_____
_____
_____

3. *ie* Words

_____
_____

night
dry
mighty
tie
fight
flight
right
might
die
spy
midnight
tonight
supply
lightning
reply
highway
high
deny
bright
sight

Say and Listen

Say each spelling word. Listen for the long *i* sound.

Think and Sort

Look at the letters in each word. Think about how long *i* is spelled. Spell each word aloud.

Long *i* can be shown as /ī/. How many spelling patterns for /ī/ do you see?

1. Look at the word *night*. The spelling pattern for this word is *igh*. The *g* and *h* are silent. Write the **thirteen** spelling words that have the *igh* pattern.

2. Write the **five** spelling words that have the *y* pattern.

3. Write the **two** spelling words that have the *ie* pattern.

Use the steps on page 6 to study words that are hard for you.

Spelling Patterns

igh	y	ie
night	**deny**	**tie**

Spelling and Meaning

Analogies   Write the spelling word that completes each analogy.

1. *In* is to *out* as *dim* is to _____.

2. *Left* is to _____ as *up* is to *down*.

3. *Weak* is to *helpless* as *strong* is to _____.

4. *Day* is to *light* as _____ is to *dark*.

5. *Rumble* is to *thunder* as *flash* is to _____.

6. *Down* is to *low* as *up* is to _____.

7. *Ear* is to *hearing* as *eye* is to _____.

8. *Gift* is to *present* as *answer* is to _____.

9. *No* is to *yes* as _____ is to *admit*.

10. *Wet* is to _____ as *hot* is to *cold*.

Definitions   Write the spelling word for each definition. Use the Spelling Dictionary if you need to.

11. the middle of the night   _____

12. to make a bow or knot   _____

13. great strength   _____

14. an airplane trip   _____

15. to struggle   _____

16. to live no more   _____

17. this night   _____

18. the amount available   _____

19. a secret agent   _____

Word Story   Long ago England's roads were called ways. Each main road was built higher than the ground around it. What was a main road called? Write the spelling word.

20. _____

Family Tree: *tie*   Think about how the *tie* words are alike in spelling and meaning. Then add another *tie* word to the tree.

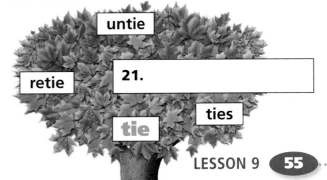

untie

retie

21.

tie

ties

The Northern Lights

If you ever visit Alaska, you _____ see an amazing

_____. Suppose that the sun has gone down and it is

a dark _____. You are riding in a car down a stretch of

_____. Suddenly there is a flash of light across the sky. It looks

like _____. The flash is so _____ that it lights up

the snow, but the light isn't white. It's green! You wonder if the strange light will

return. It does. Wavy bands of red and purple appear _____

above the clouds. Long ribbons of light touch the ground. They seem to

_____ the sky to the horizon. You cannot _____

that this is a most unusual sight. What is it? It is the Northern Lights!

Through the ages people have tried to explain the Northern Lights. Long ago

some people believed the Northern Lights were the spirits of animals or birds

in _____ . Others said the lights told whether the
        10

weather would be stormy or calm, rainy or _____ .
                                                11

Today we know that those ideas were not _____ .
                                                    12

They were only interesting stories.

Today people know what the Northern Lights really are.
They are caused by some of the most powerful forces in our solar

system. These _____ forces start on the outside
                  13

part of the sun. Huge solar flares shoot up and give off bursts
of electricity. This energy shoots toward Earth. The energy is

trapped by Earth's atmosphere. This sudden _____
                                                    14

of electric energy causes light flashes of green, red, purple,

and white.

People who want to see the Northern Lights visit a place near
the North Pole. That is the best place to see them. If a visitor asks
an expert the best way to see the lights, this might be the

_____ : "First, get away from the lights of the
   15

city. Next, _____ sleep and try to stay awake.
              16

The best lights appear around _____ . Finally,
                                      17

stay until the lights start to _____ out. That is
                                18

when beautiful clouds of light flash on and off."

Sometimes the Northern Lights stretch down and shine in other

parts of the world. If you look at the sky _____ ,
                                                19

you just might _____ a light flash. Who knows?
                  20

It could be from the Northern Lights!

night
dry
mighty
tie
fight
flight
right
might
die
spy
midnight
tonight
supply
lightning
reply
highway
high
deny
bright
sight

Spelling and Writing

- night
- dry
- mighty
- tie
- fight
- flight
- right
- might
- die
- spy
- midnight
- tonight
- supply
- lightning
- reply
- highway
- high
- deny
- bright
- sight

Write to the Point

What time of day do you like best? Write a paragraph that tells your favorite time and why you like it. Try to use spelling words from this lesson.

Use the strategies on page 7 when you are not sure how to spell a word.

Proofreading

Proofread the invitation below. Use proofreading marks to correct five spelling mistakes, three capitalization mistakes, and two unnecessary words.

Proofreading Marks
- ○ spell correctly
- ≡ capitalize
- ⌒ take out

You Are Invited!

What: a a slumber party

Where: jessica Ramon's house

When: Friday, september 5

Time: 8:00 P.M. until 9:00 A.M. Saturday

Bring: a suply of your favorite games

a sleeping bag to spend the nite

a midnigt movie—a spie or

mystery video

Please: replie to Mrs. Ramon at 888-4999

by by august 31.

Dictionary Skills

Multiple Meanings   Many words in a dictionary have more than one meaning. The Spelling Dictionary entries for *bright* and *high* give two meanings.

bright (brīt) *adj.* **bright·er, bright·est.**
1. Giving off light in large amounts:
the bright sun. **2.** Smart: *a bright child.*

high (hī) *adj.* **high·er, high·est.**
1. Extending far up; tall: *twenty feet high.*
2. Far above the ground: *a high branch.*
3. Above average: *high grades.*

Write the number of the *bright* definition that goes with each sentence.

1. My dog Baxter is very bright. _____

2. The moon is not very bright tonight. _____

3. The bright light hurt our eyes. _____

4. A bright child can solve problems quickly. _____

5. The cat's bright eyes glowed in the dark. _____

6. Following directions is always a bright idea. _____

Write the number of the *high* definition that goes with each sentence.

7. The sweater was nice, but the price was high. _____

8. The mountain is 15,000 feet high. _____

9. High diving is an Olympic event. _____

10. The car traveled at a high speed. _____

11. Three dollars is a high price for a pencil. _____

Challenge Yourself

What do you think each Challenge Word means? Check your Spelling Dictionary to see if you are right. Then use separate paper to write sentences showing that you understand the meaning of each Challenge Word.

Challenge Words
eyesight
untimely
dignify
quietness

12. Zack's poor **eyesight** made it difficult for him to see the board.

13. The **untimely** frost ruined all the fruit on the trees.

14. I won't **dignify** that silly question with a response.

15. The **quietness** of the forest relaxed me.

More Words with Long *i*

smile

1. *i*-consonant-e Words

_____
_____
_____
_____
_____
_____
_____
_____
_____
_____
_____
_____

2. *i* Words

_____
_____
_____
_____
_____
_____
_____

3. *uy* Word

_____

quiet
buy
life
knife
giant
climb
awhile
sunshine
smile
blind
slide
beside
twice
write
surprise
behind
child
size
wise
iron

Say and Listen

Say each spelling word. Listen for the long *i* sound.

Think and Sort

Look at the letters in each word. Think about how long *i* is spelled. Spell each word aloud.

Long *i* can be shown as /ī/. How many spelling patterns for /ī/ do you see?

1. Write the **twelve** spelling words that have the *i*-consonant-*e* pattern.

2. Write the **seven** spelling words that have the *i* pattern.

3. Write the **one** spelling word that has the *uy* pattern.

Use the steps on page 6 to study words that are hard for you.

Spelling Patterns

i-consonant-e	i	uy
life	child	buy

Spelling and Meaning

Definitions   Write the spelling word for each definition.

1. something that happens without warning   _____
2. of great size   _____
3. the light of the sun   _____
4. in back of   _____
5. with little or no noise   _____
6. next to   _____
7. a metal tool used to press wrinkled fabric   _____
8. for a brief time   _____
9. an instrument used for cutting   _____

Rhymes   Write the spelling word that completes each sentence and rhymes with the underlined word.

10. It's hard to _____ for a long <u>while</u>.
11. What _____ are the <u>pies</u> you baked?
12. She was so <u>nice</u> to call me _____.
13. He had a <u>wife</u> for forty years of his _____.
14. Let's _____ Dad the yellow <u>tie</u>.
15. The _____ had a <u>mild</u> cold.
16. Mike and Ike <u>tried</u> to _____ down the hill.
17. It will take a long <u>time</u> to _____ that mountain.
18. It is _____ not to tell <u>lies</u>.
19. The children were <u>kind</u> to the _____ bird.

Word Story   The Old English word *writan* meant "to outline or draw a figure of." Later the word meant "to set down in writing." Write the spelling word that comes from *writan*.

20. _____

Family Tree: *quiet*   Think about how the *quiet* words are alike in spelling and meaning. Then add another *quiet* word to the tree.

quietness

quieted

quietest

21.

quieter

quiet

BORN TO DIG!

Moles are fat little mammals that live underground. People hardly ever see them. These busy animals spend their whole _____ underground.
1

A mole is made for digging. It has a pointed nose and a V-shaped head. Its ears do not stick out, so it can _____ easily through the soil. The mole's fur flattens in either direction to allow the mole to go forward or backward in its tunnel.

The mole's best digging tools are its huge front paws. They are as strong as _____! The paws have sharp claws that cut through the soil. Then the mole uses the flat part of its paws to sweep the soil _____ it. As the mole digs, its paws move back and forth so quickly that the mole looks like a young _____ splashing in water. Moles live where there is no _____. Sight, however, is not important to moles. Moles have very tiny eyes and are almost _____.

A mole's pink mouth may have a curve that looks like a perky little _____, but this animal is not friendly at all. In fact, it likes to be alone. It is a fierce fighter, too. A small animal that falls into its

tunnel is sure to get an unhappy _____. The
9
mole senses the movement and rushes to attack. The mole grabs
the prey with its two extra-long teeth. Each curved tooth is as
sharp as a _____.
10

Most moles are between five and eight inches long.
Russian moles, however, are nearly _____ that
11
_____! These _____ moles are
12   13
very good swimmers. They like to build their tunnels
_____ a pond or river.
14

If you want to see a mole, look for a meadow that has
cone-shaped molehills. Find or _____ some
15
earthworms to drop into the mole's tunnel. Then be very still
and _____. Sit there _____. If you
16   17
are lucky, a mole will _____ up to the tunnel
18
entrance. Just remember that it is not _____ to
19
touch a mole. Its teeth and claws can hurt you!

Would you like to learn more about moles? All you need to
do is visit a library or _____ to a government
20
wildlife agency for information.

quiet
buy
life
knife
giant
climb
awhile
sunshine
smile
blind
slide
beside
twice
write
surprise
behind
child
size
wise
iron

Spelling and Writing

quiet
buy
life
knife
giant
climb
awhile
sunshine
smile
blind
slide
beside
twice
write
surprise
behind
child
size
wise
iron

Write to the Point

Write a paragraph about your favorite animal. Tell what it looks like, what it eats, and where it lives. Explain what you like about this animal, too. Try to use spelling words from this lesson.

Use the strategies on page 7 when you are not sure how to spell a word.

Proofreading

Proofread this paragraph from a report. Use proofreading marks to correct five spelling mistakes, three punctuation mistakes, and two unnecessary words.

Proofreading Marks
◯ spell correctly
⊙ add period
ℯ take out

Raccoon Report

| | |1| | |2| | |3| | |4| | |5| | |

Raccoons in the Neighborhood

You probably have a raccoon in your liffe, no matter where you live. A raccoon is a queit, furry animal with a ringed tail It might surprize you some night by your garbage can. It is a wize animal and and can figure out how to get the lid off It looks like a robber because it has a black mask across its eyes. It may run off and clime a tree. It may also sit there looking friendly. Don't think that it will make a a good pet, though It's a wild animal.

Language Connection

Nouns   A noun is a word that names a person, place, thing, or idea.
Look at the nouns below.

child   park   kite   happiness

Write the noun in each group of words.

1. giant   wise   behind

_____

2. knife   over   swam

_____

3. low   iron   before

_____

4. joy   last   twice

_____

5. beside   teach   smile

_____

6. again   child   ran

_____

7. quick   until   sunshine

_____

8. after   at   size

_____

Challenge Yourself

What do you think each Challenge Word means? Check the
Spelling Dictionary to see if you are right. Then use separate
paper to write sentences showing that you understand the
meaning of each Challenge Word.

Challenge Words	
acquire	collide
defiant	revive

9. Andy needs to earn money in order to **acquire** a new bicycle.

10. The hall is so crowded that students sometimes **collide**.

11. Rita thought her dog was **defiant** because he did not follow her commands.

12. The droopy flowers began to **revive** after the rain.

Plural Words

foxes

1. -s Plurals

_____
_____
_____
_____
_____

2. -es Plurals

_____
_____
_____
_____
_____
_____
_____
_____
_____

3. -ies Plurals

_____
_____
_____
_____
_____

brothers
families
dishes
trees
pennies
classes
pockets
cities
buses
brushes
rocks
babies
inches
branches
hikes
peaches
stories
foxes
boxes
gloves

Say and Listen

Say the spelling words. Listen to the sounds at the end of each word.

Think and Sort

All of the spelling words are plurals. **Plurals** are words that name more than one thing. Look at the spelling words. Think about how each plural was formed. Spell each word aloud.

1. Most plurals are formed by adding -*s* to the base word. Write the **six** spelling words that are formed by adding -*s*.

2. Some plurals are formed by adding -*es* to the base word. Write the **nine** spelling words that are formed by adding -*es*.

3. If a word ends in a consonant and *y*, the *y* is changed to *i* before -*es* is added. Write the **five** spelling words that are formed by dropping *y* and adding -*ies*.

Use the steps on page 6 to study words that are hard for you.

Spelling Patterns

-s	-es	-ies
trees	inches	cities
rocks	classes	stories

Spelling and Meaning

Classifying   Write the spelling word that belongs in each group.

1. planes, trains, _____
2. villages, towns, _____
3. pebbles, stones, _____
4. fathers, uncles, _____
5. dimes, nickels, _____
6. jars, cans, _____
7. yards, feet, _____
8. dogs, wolves, _____
9. leaves, twigs, _____
10. adults, children, _____
11. tales, legends, _____

What's the Answer?   Write the spelling word that answers each question.

12. What do mothers, fathers, and children belong to?   _____
13. On what do apples and oranges grow?   _____
14. What holds coins, wallets, and other things?   _____
15. What are long walks on foot?   _____
16. If it's cold, what do you wear on your hands?   _____
17. On what do people serve food?   _____
18. What do teachers call groups of students?   _____
19. What do you use on your hair and your teeth?   _____

Word Story   One of the spelling words is the name of a fruit. The Romans called this fruit a Persian apple, or *persicum malum*. The French changed the word to *pesche*. It is from *pesche* that the word came into English. Write the spelling word.

20. _____

Family Tree: *classes* *Classes* is a form of *class*. Think about how the *class* words are alike in spelling and meaning. Then add another *class* word to the tree.

classes

classify

21.

classic

class

Use each spelling word once to complete the story.

A Dream Come True

I'd always wanted to climb Harris Mountain. I'd taken _____
                                                                    1
in mountain climbing and had gone up small peaks with Jason and Michael.

They were like _____ to me. Now we were finally going to
                            2
climb the tallest mountain around these parts.

Jason, Michael, and I left early, driving through several neighboring

_____ and towns. Along the way I could hear the hum of the
        3
motors in cars and _____. Finally we arrived.
                                4
Michael said, "Come on, Small Fry."

I went, but I wanted to tell him I was tired of being called Small Fry.

We strapped ourselves together and put on our _____. I was
                                                                    5
between Michael and Jason because I cannot see.

The climb began well. The base of the mountain had lots of pines. Their

_____ felt like the bristles of _____ against
            6   7
my face. Michael described the animals he saw as we climbed—some

_____ and two rabbit _____! I heard screeching
            8   9
sounds, which Jason said came from a red-tailed hawk. We figured that her

_____ were in a nest nearby. We rested on a ledge and told
            10
_____ about exciting _____ we'd taken.
            11   12
We opened our _____ of raisins and nuts. Michael took
                            13
out the three _____
                        14
he'd packed, and we began eating.

"One good thing about this

lunch is that there are no _____ 15 _____ to wash," I joked.

Soon we began to climb again. Now there were no more pine

_____ 16 _____, just hard _____ 17 _____. Suddenly

I felt the rocks crumble beneath me and I fell. I lost all sense of

where I was and thrashed my arms and legs wildly, trying to grab

onto something. Then I remembered to stay calm.

"Are you OK?" Jason asked, holding the rope.

"Just a few more _____ 18 _____ up with your right

foot!" Michael shouted.

At last I got my footing.

"Some rock slide!" yelled Michael. "Nice work, Nick!"

The rest of the way up the mountain was easier. At the top I

searched my _____ 19 _____ until I found the three lucky

_____ 20 _____ that Jason had given me, knowing that it was

more than luck that got us to the top. I placed the coins on the

ground as proof that we were there.

Somehow I knew, too, that they would never call

me Small Fry again.

brothers
families
dishes
trees
pennies
classes
pockets
cities
buses
brushes
rocks
babies
inches
branches
hikes
peaches
stories
foxes
boxes
gloves

Spelling and Writing

brothers
families
dishes
trees
pennies
classes
pockets
cities
buses
brushes
rocks
babies
inches
branches
hikes
peaches
stories
foxes
boxes
gloves

Write to the Point

Nick's mountain climb had some scary moments, but afterward he was proud. Have you ever learned how to do something that was scary at first? Write a paragraph about what it was like. Try to use spelling words from this lesson.

Use the strategies on page 7 when you are not sure how to spell a word.

Proofreading

Proofread the newspaper article below. Use proofreading marks to correct five spelling mistakes, three punctuation mistakes, and two missing words.

Proofreading Marks
◯ spell correctly
⊙ add period
∧ add

Outdoor Life

Outdoor Fun in the City
by Mark Swift

Many famillys living in citys can't take hiks in the woods They have to visit parks to enjoy nature. Many parks have trees and rockes climb. They also have wild animals such rabbits and squirrels to watch Many animal babyes are born in the spring. It's the perfect season for enjoying park wildlife

Language Connection

Subject of a Sentence   The subject of a sentence is the person or thing that is doing the action or is being talked about. To find the subject, first find the predicate. Then ask yourself who or what does the action in the predicate. The answer is the subject of the sentence. In the sentence below, *marched past the palace* is the predicate, so *The brave soldiers* is the subject of the sentence.

> **The brave soldiers** marched past the palace.

Write the subject of each sentence below.

1. Peaches grow on the tree in my grandmother's front yard.

   _____

2. Her older brothers go to high school.

   _____

3. Two cardboard boxes tumbled off the shelf.

   _____

4. Dance classes begin at three o'clock.

   _____

5. My aunt's twin babies look exactly alike.

   _____

6. The oak trees lost their leaves in October.

   _____

Challenge Yourself

What do you think each Challenge Word means? Check the Spelling Dictionary to see if you are right. Then use separate paper to write sentences showing that you understand the meaning of each Challenge Word.

Challenge Words	
utensils	draperies
skiers	festivities

7. Fog hid the mountain like **draperies** covering a window.
8. Many **skiers** race down the mountain slopes after it snows.
9. Our only cooking **utensils** were a pan and a spoon.
10. The party's **festivities** included singing and special foods.

Lesson 12

Unit 2 Review
Lessons 7–11

Use the steps on page 6 to study words that are hard for you.

7

secret
family
evening
people
radio
police

More Words with Long e

Write the spelling word for each clue.

1. Your cousins, uncles, and aunts are part of this group. _____
2. This is something you should keep. _____
3. This plays music. _____
4. This time of day happens after sunset. _____
5. All men, women, and children make up this group. _____
6. These people protect our communities. _____

8

picture
interesting
different
gym
package
building

Words with Short i

Write the spelling word for each definition.

7. a room used for playing sports _____
8. a place with offices where people work _____
9. not the same _____
10. a box or bundle containing something _____
11. holding one's attention _____
12. a photo, painting, or drawing _____

9

lightning
tonight
supply
tie

Words with Long *i*

Write the spelling word that belongs in each group.

13. rain, thunder, _____

14. coat, shirt, _____

15. today, tomorrow, _____

16. give, provide, _____

10

surprise
quiet
climb
buy

More Words with Long *i*

Write the spelling word that is a synonym for each underlined word or words.

17. You should be <u>silent</u> during a movie. _____

18. Eva wants to <u>purchase</u> that watch. _____

19. The two boys will <u>move up</u> the playground ladders.

_____

20. Imagine my <u>amazement</u> when I saw
you! _____

11

brothers
inches
families
pennies
babies

Plural Words

Write the spelling word that completes each analogy.

21. *Ones* is to *hundreds* as _____ is to *dollars*.

22. *Does* is to *fawns* as *mothers* is to _____.

23. *Meters* is to *centimeters* as *yards* is to _____.

24. *Girls* is to *sisters* as *boys* is to _____.

25. *Dens* is to *lions* as *houses* is to _____.

26. /ē/ Words

_____

_____

_____

_____

_____

27. /ĭ/ Words

_____

_____

_____

_____

_____

_____

_____

28. /ī/ Words

_____

_____

_____

_____

_____

_____

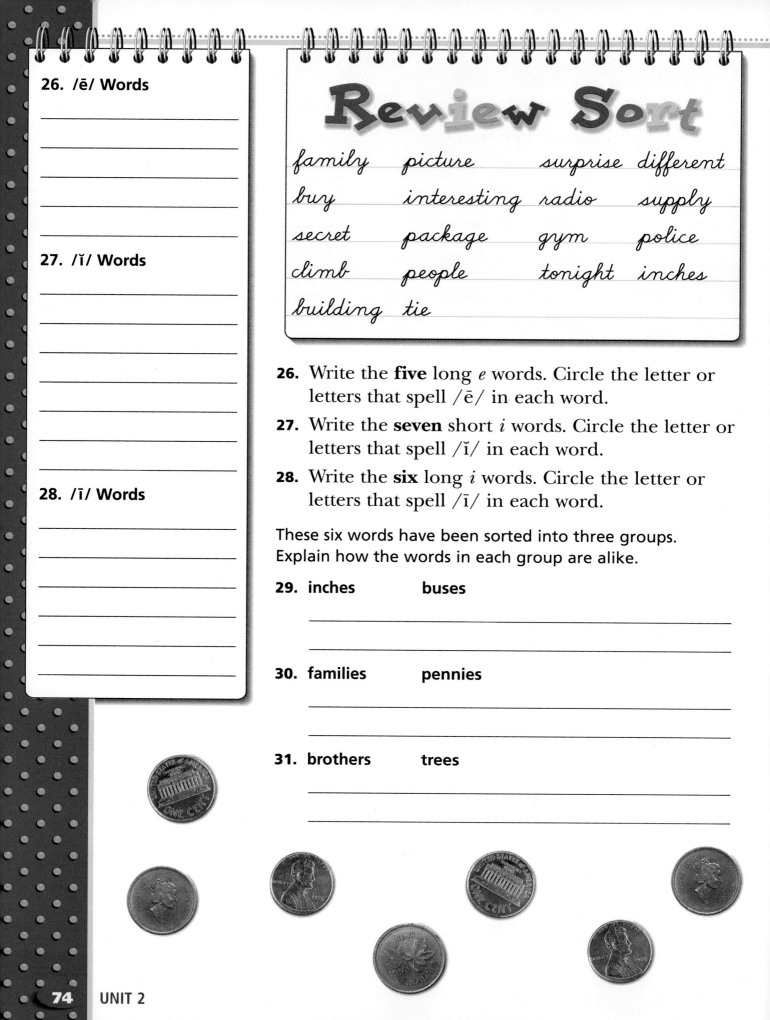

Review Sort

family	picture	surprise	different
buy	interesting	radio	supply
secret	package	gym	police
climb	people	tonight	inches
building	tie		

26. Write the **five** long _e_ words. Circle the letter or letters that spell /ē/ in each word.

27. Write the **seven** short _i_ words. Circle the letter or letters that spell /ĭ/ in each word.

28. Write the **six** long _i_ words. Circle the letter or letters that spell /ī/ in each word.

These six words have been sorted into three groups. Explain how the words in each group are alike.

29. inches   buses

_____

_____

30. families   pennies

_____

_____

31. brothers   trees

_____

_____

Writer's Workshop

A Narrative

A narrative is a story that can be true or made-up. A made-up story is called fiction. It comes from a writer's imagination. A good narrative grabs the reader's interest at the beginning of the story. Then it keeps the reader wondering what will happen next. Here is the beginning of Koji's story about a boy who loses his brother's skateboard.

Prewriting To write his narrative, Koji followed the steps in the writing process. After he decided on an idea for his story, he completed a story map. The story map helped Koji plan his narrative. He wrote down each important event that would take place in the story. Part of Koji's story map is shown here. Study what Koji did.

> The Lost Skateboard
>
> It was truly the most wonderful skateboard Matt had ever seen. It was shiny red, and the new wheels spun quietly and smoothly. Matt's big brother, Andy, had been given the skateboard for his birthday only last week.
>
> "Can I borrow your skateboard?" Matt asked.
>
> "I guess so. Just make sure you don't let anything happen to it," Andy said.

Beginning

Matt borrows his big brother's new skateboard.

Middle

Matt leaves skateboard on the bus.

It's Your Turn!

Write your own narrative. You can write a story like Koji's, a fairy tale, or any other kind of story you wish. Once you have your story idea, make a story map to plan the main events. Then follow the other steps in the writing process—writing, revising, proofreading, and publishing. Try to use spelling words from this lesson in your narrative.

Words with Short o

doctor

1. o Words

_____
_____
_____
_____
_____
_____
_____
_____
_____
_____
_____
_____
_____
_____

2. a Words

_____
_____
_____
_____

hobby
wash
model
forgot
doctor
contest
object
o'clock
wallet
cotton
dollar
solve
watch
knock
problem
bottom
swallow
beyond
knot
hospital

Say and Listen

Say each spelling word. Listen for the short o sound.

Think and Sort

Look at the letters in each word. Think about how short o is spelled. Spell each word aloud.

Short o can be shown as /ŏ/. How many spelling patterns for /ŏ/ do you see?

1. Write the **sixteen** spelling words that have the o pattern.

2. Write the **four** spelling words that have the a pattern.

> Use the steps on page 6 to study words that are hard for you.

Spelling Patterns

o	a
s**o**lve	w**a**sh

Spelling and Meaning

Classifying   Write the spelling word that belongs in each group.

1. sparrow, wren, _____

2. tap, _____, bang

3. clean, scrub, _____

4. see, _____, observe

5. dime, quarter, _____

6. unscramble, answer, _____

7. _____, silk, wool

8. race, game, _____

9. goal, _____, purpose

10. billfold, _____, purse

11. example, _____, copy

12. past, over, _____

What's the Answer?   Write the spelling word that answers each question.

13. Whom do people call when they are sick?   _____

14. What is the opposite of *remembered*?   _____

15. What word means "of the clock"?   _____

16. What can be tied in a rope or cord?   _____

17. What is the opposite of *top*?   _____

18. Stamp collecting is an example of what?   _____

19. What comes before a solution?   _____

Word Story   *Hospitale* was a Latin word that meant "guesthouse." Write the spelling word that comes from *hospitale* and now means "a place where sick people go to get well."

20. _____

Family Tree: *wash*   Think about how the *wash* words are alike in spelling and meaning. Then add another *wash* word to the tree.

washing

washer

rewash

21.

washable

washes

wash

Use each spelling word once to complete the story.

A Hobby for Angela

My sister just built a _____ 1 of a ship. Building models is

her _____ 2 . My brother likes to work with leather. He made a

beautiful _____ 3 last week. Dad gave him a _____ 4

to put in it. Dad was happy because he finally won a _____ 5 . He's

always entering them. I thought the contest he won was silly. Dad wrote 25 words

about why he likes to do the _____ 6 with new blue Cleano. And

Mom? She likes to _____ 7 birds. She was very excited Monday

when she saw a _____ 8 .

I'm the only one in my family who doesn't have a hobby. Everyone else has

one thing that he or she loves to do. My _____ 9 is that I like

everything. It seems a shame to spend all my time on one activity. There are so

many interesting things to do. Yesterday I even got into a "scrape" trying to

_____ 10 my hobby problem.

It all started when I thought skating might be my hobby. I was rolling down

Holly Hill and had just picked up speed. The wind felt wonderful against my face.

Then I saw someone flying a kite at the park. The kite was made of bright blue

_____ 11 fabric. Red tails were waving below it. Each tail had a

bow-tie _____ 12 tied at the end

of it. I _____ 13 all about skating.

I thought about how much fun flying kites would

be as a hobby. Before I knew it, I was at the _____

14

of the hill. Just _____ the bottom is a sharp turn.

15

Well, the road turned, but I didn't. CRASH! My right knee got quite

a _____, and I got a scrape on my chin.

16

Mom wasn't too happy when the police officer called her at

two _____. She left her office and met us at the

17

_____. At first she was angry with me. Then

18

she told me she was only angry because she was frightened.

The _____ cleaned my scrape and bandaged

19

my knee. She told me to wash my chin with special medicine.

I didn't _____. My chin hurt, and I wanted to

20

get better.

It was an exciting day, though. I got to see lots of doctors and

nurses. The inside of a hospital is really interesting. I told the doctor

how much I liked visiting the hospital. Mom couldn't stop laughing

when the doctor said, "Just don't make it a hobby!"

hobby
wash
model
forgot
doctor
contest
object
o'clock
wallet
cotton
dollar
solve
watch
knock
problem
bottom
swallow
beyond
knot
hospital

Spelling and Writing

hobby
wash
model
forgot
doctor
contest
object
o'clock
wallet
cotton
dollar
solve
watch
knock
problem
bottom
swallow
beyond
knot
hospital

Write to the Point

Angela wanted a hobby but couldn't decide on one. Write a paragraph about your favorite hobby or one that you would enjoy. Tell what makes it interesting or fun. Try to use spelling words from this lesson.

Use the strategies on page 7 when you are not sure how to spell a word.

Proofreading

Proofread the contest announcement below. Use proofreading marks to correct five spelling mistakes, three capitalization mistakes, and two punctuation mistakes.

Proofreading Marks
◯ spell correctly
≡ capitalize
⊙ add period

Model Plane Contest

Do you build model planes for a hobbie?

enter this contest and win a fifty-dollar

prize! You can also win a new leather walet

or a cool wotch. Fill out the form at the

bottom of this page Bring your completed

form and your plane to the school gym by

ten oclock friday morning.

anyone can enter

Dictionary Skills

Parts of Speech   A dictionary lists the part of speech for each entry word. For example, a word may be a noun (*n.*) or a verb (*v.*). Most dictionaries abbreviate the part of speech. Here are some common abbreviations for the parts of speech.

noun **n.**	adjective **adj.**	preposition **prep.**	verb **v.**	adverb **adv.**

Write the following words in alphabetical order. Look up each word in the Spelling Dictionary and write its part of speech.

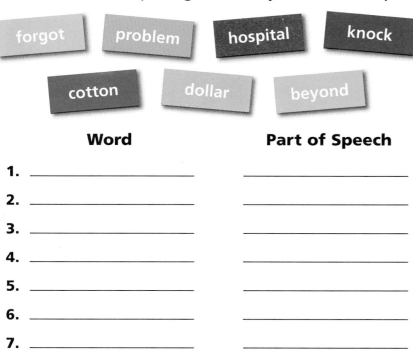

forgot   problem   hospital   knock

cotton   dollar   beyond

EMERGENCY

Word	Part of Speech
1. _____	_____
2. _____	_____
3. _____	_____
4. _____	_____
5. _____	_____
6. _____	_____
7. _____	_____

Challenge Yourself

Use the Spelling Dictionary to answer the questions. Then use separate paper to write sentences showing that you understand the meaning of each Challenge Word.

Challenge Words

squad	exotic
apricot	volcanic

8. Would you expect to find a **squad** of players on a field during a football game?   _____

9. Would you expect to see **exotic** birds and animals from around the world at a famous zoo?   _____

10. Does an **apricot** look like a banana?   _____

11. After the fire goes out, would you expect to find **volcanic** ashes in your fireplace?   _____

Words with Long *o*

pony

1. *o* Words

_____
_____
_____
_____
_____
_____
_____
_____
_____
_____
_____
_____
_____

2. *oa* Words

_____
_____
_____
_____
_____

3. *oe* Words

_____
_____

clothes
total
oak
ocean
obey
throat
pony
poem
coach
coast
goes
almost
only
comb
motor
hotel
soap
zero
toe
program

Say and Listen

Say each spelling word. Listen for the long *o* sound.

Think and Sort

Look at the letters in each word. Think about how long *o* is spelled. Spell each word aloud.

Long *o* can be shown as /ō/. How many spelling patterns for /ō/ do you see?

1. Write the **thirteen** spelling words that have the *o* pattern.

2. Write the **five** spelling words that have the *oa* pattern.

3. Write the **two** spelling words that have the *oe* pattern.

Use the steps on page 6 to study words that are hard for you.

Spelling Patterns

o	oa	oe
zero	soap	goes

Spelling and Meaning

Synonyms Write the spelling word that is a synonym for each underlined word.

1. This <u>shoreline</u> is rocky and steep. _____
2. Wally <u>nearly</u> lost the race. _____
3. You must <u>follow</u> the rules to play. _____
4. The <u>sum</u> was more than fifty dollars. _____
5. Collin <u>travels</u> everywhere by bus. _____
6. The <u>sea</u> here is very blue. _____
7. Ramon had <u>just</u> five dollars left. _____
8. What is your favorite TV <u>show</u>? _____

Clues Write the spelling word for each clue.

9. People wash with this. _____
10. Ten minus ten equals this. _____
11. This is a place for travelers to stay. _____
12. This is a small horse. _____
13. You can use this to make your hair neat. _____
14. This can get sore when you get a cold. _____
15. This can rhyme. _____
16. This is found on your foot. _____
17. This is a kind of tree. _____
18. This person trains athletes. _____
19. People wear these. _____

Word Story Many English words come from Latin. One of the spelling words and the word *move* come from the same Latin word, *movere*. The spelling word names a machine that causes things to move. Write the word.

20. _____

Family Tree: *comb* Think about how the *comb* words are alike in spelling and meaning. Then add another *comb* word to the tree.

combed
uncombed
21.
combs
comb

Spelling in Context Use each spelling word once to complete the selection.

Vacation Mail

Dear Grandma,

  We've been on vacation in Grand Cayman for _____ [1] a week now. Our _____ [2] is nice. They give you little bars of face _____ [3] and little bottles of shampoo.

  The most fun I've had so far is snorkeling in the _____ [4]. Dad decided to take me with him after we'd been here for _____ [5] one day. I had to promise to _____ [6] the safety rules at all times! Dad taught me how to move the funny rubber feet. Then I learned to breathe through a snorkel.

  Later that afternoon, we went along the _____ [7] by boat to a coral reef. When we turned the _____ [8] off and stopped the boat, Dad and another diver jumped over the side. Then I went in, yelling, "Here _____ [9] nothing!"

  I swam near the surface. A beautiful angelfish swam right in front of my face. A canary fish brushed my side. My feeling was one of _____ [10] wonder. I am going to write a _____ [11] about swimming with the fish.

  Dad had to drag me out of the water. Then we changed out of our swimsuits and into our _____ [12] and got the other diver to take a picture of us. Can you tell that we forgot to _____ [13] our hair? I got a sore _____ [14], but it was worth it!

        Love,

        Tracy

84   UNIT 3

Dear Tracy,

How lucky you are to be on Grand Cayman! This morning the temperature here fell to _____, and my old _____ tree is totally covered with snow. Outside, Mr. Johnson's _____ is puffing his white breath into the air. I am stuck indoors for a while—I tripped and broke my _____ yesterday.

I loved your letter. The picture of you and your dad is very funny! I'll bet snorkeling is really fun. I've never been, but I watched a _____ about it on television last month.

Well, hurry home! I found out I will be the _____ of the Hillsboro soccer team. We start practice next week. By then I will be able to walk. Why not come with me to practice?

Love you,

Grandma

15
16
17
18
19
20

clothes
total
oak
ocean
obey
throat
pony
poem
coach
coast
goes
almost
only
comb
motor
hotel
soap
zero
toe
program

Spelling and Writing

clothes
total
oak
ocean
obey
throat
pony
poem
coach
coast
goes
almost
only
comb
motor
hotel
soap
zero
toe
program

Write to the Point

Is there a person you are close to but don't see very often? Write a short letter to that person, telling him or her some of the news in your life. You might want to share a special event, something funny, or your plans for a future trip. Try to use spelling words from this lesson.

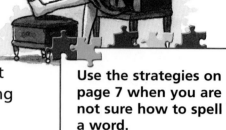

Use the strategies on page 7 when you are not sure how to spell a word.

Proofreading

Proofread the journal entry below. Use proofreading marks to correct five spelling mistakes, three capitalization mistakes, and two unnecessary words.

Proofreading Marks
◯ spell correctly
≡ capitalize
✐ take out

august 23

Our vacation at the coest has been so much fun.

our hotal room overlooks the ocean. Every

morning i run to to the beach for a swim. Today I

stuck only my toa in the water. It was too cold to

swim. If it doesn't warm up, Dad and I can still

combe the the beach for seashells. Our vacation

is allmost over, but it's been great.

Language Connection

Capital Letters   Use a capital letter to begin a person's first and last names. Also use a capital letter to begin a title that goes with someone's name.

> Mrs. Emerick works in the school cafeteria.
>
> Barry and Judy both play sports.

The sentences below contain errors in capitalization. Write each sentence correctly.

1. laurie, amber, and keisha climbed to the top of the rope.

_____

_____

2. miss santucci said that the ropes feel as if they've been coated with soap.

_____

_____

3. On Tuesday we have basketball practice with mr. dowling.

_____

_____

4. rebecca and jamal keep track of the points that each team scores.

_____

_____

⭐ Challenge Yourself

Write the correct Challenge Word for each clue. Check the Spelling Dictionary to see if you are right. Then use separate paper to write sentences showing that you understand the meaning of each Challenge Word.

Challenge Words

appropriate	host
enclosure	foe

5. You can use this to keep a pet from running away. _____

6. This word rhymes with *ghost* and means "a person who entertains guests." _____

7. An enemy is this. _____

8. If you dress warmly on a very cold day, then your clothing is this. _____

More Words with Long *o*

window

1. *o*-consonant-*e* Words

_____
_____
_____
_____
_____
_____
_____
_____
_____

2. *ow* Words

_____
_____
_____
_____
_____
_____
_____
_____
_____
_____

3. *ough* Word

_____

below
elbow
froze
alone
broke
though
knows
pillow
own
explode
hollow
chose
shadow
close
nose
those
slowly
tomorrow
stole
window

Say and Listen

Say each spelling word. Listen for the long *o* sound.

Think and Sort

Look at the letters in each word. Think about how long *o* is spelled. Spell each word aloud.

Long *o* can be shown as /ō/. How many spelling patterns for /ō/ do you see?

1. Write the **nine** spelling words that have the *o*-consonant-*e* pattern.

2. Write the **ten** spelling words that have the *ow* pattern.

3. In the *ough* spelling pattern, the *g* and the *h* are silent. Write the **one** spelling word that has the *ough* pattern.

> Use the steps on page 6 to study words that are hard for you.

Spelling Patterns

o-consonant-e	ow	ough
broke	own	though

Spelling and Meaning

Antonyms   Write the spelling word that is an antonym of each underlined word.

1. The trunk of the oak tree was <u>solid</u>. _____
2. Dad <u>fixed</u> the new window. _____
3. Will you please <u>open</u> the door? _____
4. The car drove <u>quickly</u> past the house. _____
5. Aunt Cleo <u>thawed</u> the turkey. _____
6. Todd's apartment is <u>above</u> Yuri's. _____
7. Let's do the assignment <u>together</u>. _____

Analogies   Write the spelling word that completes each analogy.

8. *Eat* is to *ate* as *steal* is to _____.
9. *Board* is to *hard* as _____ is to *soft*.
10. *Leg* is to *knee* as *arm* is to _____.
11. *Sing* is to *sang* as *choose* is to _____.
12. *Yesterday* is to *past* as _____ is to *future*.
13. *Taste* is to *mouth* as *smell* is to _____.
14. *Says* is to *speaks* as _____ is to *understands*.
15. *Match* is to *burn* as *firecracker* is to _____.
16. *Dark* is to _____ as *smooth* is to *silk*.
17. *Hard* is to *difficult* as *have* is to _____.
18. *This* is to *that* as *these* is to _____.
19. *Also* is to *too* as _____ is to *however*.

Word Story   One of the spelling words comes from the old Viking word *vindauga. Vindauga* meant "wind-eye." A *vindauga* was an opening, through which the wind might enter a house. Today this opening is often covered with glass. Write the word.

20. _____

Family Tree: own   Think about how the *own* words are alike in spelling and meaning. Then add another *own* word to the tree.

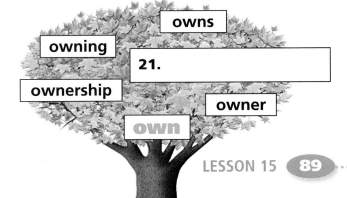

owns

owning

21.

ownership

owner

own

Pop's Old Barn

The old barn on the Wilson farm stood on the hilltop and cast a long black

_____ . Moonlight streaming through each _____
　　　　　　1　　　　　　　　　　　　　　　　　　　　　　　　　　　2

made it look like a _____ head. People said that the barn was
　　　　　　　　　　　　　3

haunted. Young John Wilson agreed. "Count me out if you're going to Pop's old

barn," he told his friends.

"I don't think that place is scary," B.J. said. "Do you, Sarah?"

"No, I don't," Sarah answered firmly.

"I want to explore the barn _____ night. Who's going with
　　　　　　　　　　　　　　　　　4

me?" asked B.J.

Sarah thought for a minute, then _____ to join B.J. "I will!"
　　　　　　　　　　　　　　　　　　　　　　5

she replied.

But John said, "I wish my pop would tear it down. Count me out."

Late the next evening, B.J. and Sarah quietly _____ through
　　　　　　　　　　　　　　　　　　　　　　　　　　　6

the Wilson land to the barn. _____ they removed a wooden
　　　　　　　　　　　　　　　　　7

bolt from the door. The squeaking noise made their skin crawl. Standing very

_____ together, they tiptoed through the pitch-black room.
　　　　　8

Rustling noises came from in front of them.

"I wonder what _____ noises are," B.J. said. Then he felt
　　　　　　　　　　　　9

something brush his shoe. He _____ in his tracks. His hands felt
　　　　　　　　　　　　　　　　　　10

as _____ they were made of ice. "Something just hit
　　　11

my foot," he whispered.

"It was probably just a mouse," Sarah said shakily. Then she looked around. "Maybe we should go home," she told B.J. "Who _____ 12 _____ what's inside this place?"

"No, let's go on," B.J. said. "I want to find out if this place is really haunted." He took Sarah by an _____ 13 _____ and led her to a ladder just _____ 14 _____ the loft.

As they began to climb, they heard a crack. A rung of the ladder _____ 15 _____ beneath B.J.'s foot, sending him falling to the ground. He dusted himself off and got up. "Look!" he cried.

A strange purple light was circling the room. B.J. and Sarah stared at a pale white face as a wild laugh filled the barn.

"Help!" Sarah screamed. Then she ran like a scared rabbit.

B.J. answered with a scream of his _____ 16 _____. "Sarah, don't leave me here _____ 17 _____!" His voice seemed to _____ 18 _____ from inside him. He shot toward the door. Suddenly the white face was right in front of him!

"Hey, guys, it's me!" said John. He tossed off a white case from a _____ 19 _____. In it he had cut holes for his eyes and _____ 20 _____. He circled his flashlight once more around the room.

"Was I pretty scary?" he asked with a laugh.

B.J. and Sarah looked at each other and giggled. "Yes!" they said together. "Too scary!"

below
elbow
froze
alone
broke
though
knows
pillow
own
explode
hollow
chose
shadow
close
nose
those
slowly
tomorrow
stole
window

Spelling and Writing

Use the strategies on page 7 when you are not sure how to spell a word.

below
elbow
froze
alone
broke
though
knows
pillow
own
explode
hollow
chose
shadow
close
nose
those
slowly
tomorrow
stole
window

Write to the Point

The story "Pop's Old Barn" contains details that describe the barn. Write a paragraph describing a place that you know well. It may be your bedroom, the attic, the cellar, or a place outdoors. Include details that tell what you hear, see, smell, and feel when you are there. Try to use spelling words from this lesson.

Proofreading

Proofread this paragraph from a book jacket. Use proofreading marks to correct five spelling mistakes, three capitalization mistakes, and two punctuation mistakes.

Proofreading Marks

◯ spell correctly
≡ capitalize
? add question mark

One night Mario sat at the desk in his room. suddenly he frose. Did something move near the windoe Mario felt as thogh his heart would explode. Then he laughed. It was only his shaddow. Mario laid his head on his pillow and sloly fell asleep. then a loud knock at the front door woke him. who would be visiting at this time of night The book *House on the Hill* will keep you reading as the mystery unfolds.

Language Connection

Quotation Marks Place quotation marks around the exact words of a speaker. Sometimes these words are at the end of a sentence. Sometimes they are at the beginning.

> Robin said, **"I'm going to the dentist tomorrow."**
>
> **"Did you hear the fireworks explode?"** asked Raoul.

Rewrite the following sentences, using quotation marks correctly.

1. Bob said, The door to the cellar froze shut.

_____

2. My model car broke! yelled Michael.

_____

3. Is something living in that hollow log? asked Delia.

_____

4. Zak yelled, Look at your shadow on the wall!

_____

5. Stay close together as we hike, said the guide.

_____

6. Randi asked, Is this pillow made of feathers?

_____

Challenge Yourself

What do you think each Challenge Word means? Check the Spelling Dictionary to see if you are right. Then use separate paper to write sentences showing that you understand the meaning of each Challenge Word.

Challenge Words	
bouquet	dispose
stow	sow

7. The flowers were made into a beautiful **bouquet**.

8. Please use the garbage can to **dispose** of your trash.

9. Passengers must **stow** their suitcases under their seats or in a closet.

10. In spring we **sow** grass seed on our front lawn.

Words with Short *u*

jungle

1. *u* Words

_____
_____
_____
_____
_____
_____
_____
_____
_____
_____
_____

2. *ou* Words

_____
_____
_____
_____
_____
_____
_____
_____

3. *oe* Word

_____

suddenly
rough
knuckle
trouble
touch
brush
couple
button
does
fudge
hunt
enough
tough
country
until
double
subject
under
jungle
hundred

Say and Listen

Say each spelling word. Listen for the short *u* sound.

Think and Sort

Look at the letters in each word. Think about how short *u* is spelled. Spell each word aloud.

Short *u* can be shown as /ŭ/. How many spelling patterns for /ŭ/ do you see?

1. Write the **eleven** spelling words that have the *u* pattern.

2. Write the **eight** spelling words that have the *ou* pattern.

3. Write the **one** spelling word that has the *oe* pattern.

Use the steps on page 6 to study words that are hard for you.

Spelling Patterns

u	ou	oe
hunt	touch	does

Spelling and Meaning

Hink Pinks   Hink pinks are pairs of rhyming words that have a funny meaning. Read each meaning. Write the spelling word that completes each hink pink.

1. grooming the hair in a hurry   _____ rush
2. things made out of sandpaper   _____ stuff
3. looking for a daring trick to do   stunt _____
4. person choosing the best candy   _____ judge
5. something that fastens fingers together   _____ buckle
6. twins who always cause problems   _____ trouble
7. a piece of meat that is hard to chew   _____ stuff

What's the Answer?   Write the spelling word that answers each question.

8. Where are you looking when you look below something? _____
9. Which word is a form of *do*?   _____
10. What is science or math an example of?   _____
11. Which word means "up to the time of"?   _____
12. What is Canada?   _____
13. How many pennies are in a dollar?   _____
14. What can you call two things?   _____
15. What is another word for *difficulty*?   _____
16. To which sense do fingers belong?   _____
17. Which word means "to happen without warning"? _____
18. What do you have when you have all you need? _____
19. What place is hot and wet?   _____

Word Story   The French word for a flower bud is *bouton*. One spelling word comes from *bouton*. It names a knob that pushes through a buttonhole like a flower bud pushes through leaves. Write the spelling word.

20. _____

Family Tree: *rough*   Think about how the *rough* words are alike in spelling and meaning. Then add another *rough* word to the tree.

- rougher
- roughly
- 21.
- roughened
- roughen
- **rough**

Use each spelling word once to complete the story.

The Oral Report

Jenna was scared. She stared at the clock in Mr. Olivero's room. Only twenty more minutes _____ 1 lunch! By then all this would be over.

"Maybe he'll forget about it," Jenna wished. "I'll bet there isn't _____ 2 time to hear everyone today, anyway."

Jenna started to _____ 3 through her desk for her notes. Mr. Olivero began, "The _____ 4 of this week's geography lesson is South America. We are going to hear some reports from our Brazil team. _____ 5 the team have everything in order?"

"Yes, Mr. Olivero," said Patrick Johnson.

Jenna stared down at her notes. It was almost her turn. One of her fingernails felt _____ 6. She chewed it nervously.

Jenna felt Patrick _____ 7 past her as he stepped to the front of the room. She was surprised to see Patrick's hands shaking. Poor Patrick was holding his notes so tightly that each _____ 8 on his hands was white!

"Brazil," he began. "Brazil is the largest _____ 9 in South America. Its population is more than _____ 10 that of other South American countries. . . ."

Jenna barely heard Patrick's speech as she nervously played with a loose _____ 11 on her dress. She thought about the big piece of _____ 12 cake that she would eat at lunch. Jenna looked at the clock again. In a _____ 13 of minutes, the bell would ring.

"Very nice, Patrick. And now, we will hear from Jenna about the Amazon River."

Jenna's heart pounded. Her wet, shaking hands reached _____ her desk for the map she had made for
14
the report.

"Oh, no. Where's my map?" she wondered. "I guess I'm really in _____ now!" _____ she
15   16
felt her fingers _____ the map. Jenna stepped
17
to the front of the room.

"The Amazon River begins in the Andes Mountains and flows eastward through Brazil," she said loudly. "More than two _____ small rivers flow into the Amazon.
18
Much of the land along the river is _____ . . . ."
19

Before she knew it, the report was done and the bell rang. Patrick ran up to Jenna. "That wasn't as _____
20
as we thought it would be!" he told her.

Then Anna Ramos joined them. "Hey, guys. You were great! Were you scared?"

"Are you kidding?" laughed Jenna. "It was nothing!"

suddenly
rough
knuckle
trouble
touch
brush
couple
button
does
fudge
hunt
enough
tough
country
until
double
subject
under
jungle
hundred

Amazon R.

Amazon River Brazil

BRAZIL

Spelling and Writing

suddenly
rough
knuckle
trouble
touch
brush
couple
button
does
fudge
hunt
enough
tough
country
until
double
subject
under
jungle
hundred

Write to the Point

Like Jenna, most people feel nervous before giving an oral report. Have you ever given an oral report? What advice would you give others to help them make sure that their report goes smoothly? Write a list of things they can do before and during their speech. Try to use spelling words from this lesson.

Use the strategies on page 7 when you are not sure how to spell a word.

Proofreading

Proofread the e-mail below. Use proofreading marks to correct five spelling mistakes, three capitalization mistakes, and two punctuation mistakes.

Proofreading Marks

◯ spell correctly
≡ capitalize
? add question mark

---

e-mail

| Address Book | Attachment | Check Spelling | Send | Save Draft | Cancel |

Libby,

Is your oral report due next week I hope the work won't be too tuff. What is your report about I might be able to help if you need me.

I have untill friday to prepare a rough draft of my oral report on Martin luther King, Jr. I chose dr. King because he was such a great leader of his contry. I had no trubble finding enogh information.

Bridget

Dictionary Skills

Pronunciation A dictionary lists the pronunciation for most entry words. A pronunciation is written with letters and special symbols. The symbols are a guide to the sounds of the word.

> **e·nough** (ĭ nŭf′) *adj.* Sufficient to satisfy a need: *enough money for the movie.*

Write the following words in alphabetical order. Then look up each word in the Spelling Dictionary and write its pronunciation beside it.

hundred   couple   rough   touch

1. _____ _____

2. _____ _____

3. _____ _____

4. _____ _____

Write the spelling word that each pronunciation represents. Then check your answers in the Spelling Dictionary.

5. /tŭf/ _____   6. /kŭn′ trē/ _____

7. /nŭk′ əl/ _____   8. /sŭb′ jĭkt/ _____

9. /sŭd′n lē/ _____   10. /ĭ nŭf′/ _____

Challenge Yourself

Use the Spelling Dictionary to answer the questions. Then use separate paper to write sentences showing that you understand the meaning of each Challenge Word.

Challenge Words

customary
countryside
erupt
construct

11. Is it **customary** for students to study for tests at a party? _____

12. Would a book about volcanoes probably tell why they **erupt**? _____

13. Would it be wise to **construct** a boat out of paper? _____

14. Would the **countryside** be a good place to find insects and wildflowers?

_____

Contractions

couldn't

1. Contractions with *not*

_____
_____
_____
_____
_____
_____
_____
_____
_____
_____
_____
_____

2. Other Contractions

a. _____

b. _____

c. _____

d. _____

e. _____

f. _____

g. _____

h. _____

that's
she'd
they've
weren't
doesn't
isn't
wouldn't
wasn't
aren't
we're
you'd
don't
I'm
hadn't
haven't
didn't
shouldn't
let's
couldn't
they'll

Say and Listen

Say the spelling words. Listen to the ending sounds.

Think and Sort

All of the spelling words are contractions. A **contraction** is a short way to write two or more words. The words are joined, but one or more letters are left out. An apostrophe (') is used in place of the missing letters. Look at each spelling word. Think about what the second word in the contraction is. Spell each word aloud.

1. Write the **twelve** spelling words that are contractions formed with *not*.

2. Solve these contraction puzzles to write **eight** spelling words.

   a. I + am =   **b.** that + is =

   c. we + are =   **d.** let + us =

   e. they + have = **f.** you + would =

   g. she + had =   **h.** they + will =

Use the steps on page 6 to study words that are hard for you.

Spelling Patterns

do + not = don't	they + have = they've	you + had = you'd you + would = you'd

Spelling and Meaning

Rhymes   Write the spelling word that completes each sentence and rhymes with the underlined word.

1. When the bells <u>chime</u>, _____ going home.
2. The team made a <u>save</u>, and now _____ won!
3. She said that _____ <u>need</u> your help.
4. Soon _____ going to move <u>near</u> you.
5. Maybe _____ like to eat Chinese <u>food</u>.
6. After the sun <u>sets</u>, _____ take a walk.
7. Tomorrow _____ pick up the <u>mail</u>.
8. I guess _____ the last of the <u>hats</u>.
9. They _____ going to eat <u>burnt</u> toast.

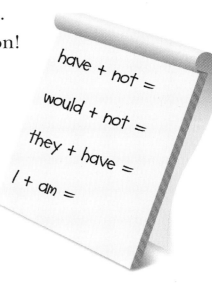

Trading Places   Write the spelling word that can take the place of the underlined words in each sentence.

10. Wanda <u>did not</u> plan a fancy party.   _____
11. We <u>do not</u> want to argue.   _____
12. This pen <u>does not</u> leak.   _____
13. The bus <u>was not</u> on time today.   _____
14. The students <u>have not</u> eaten lunch yet.   _____
15. I <u>would not</u> try to trick you.   _____
16. You <u>should not</u> forget to brush your teeth.   _____
17. Broccoli <u>is not</u> my favorite vegetable.   _____
18. My parents <u>are not</u> able to go to the meeting.   _____
19. We <u>had not</u> seen the new baby before today.   _____

Word Story   Verbs have different forms for present, past, and future actions. A form of the verb *can* used to be spelled *colde*. Guess how we spell *colde* today. Then add *not* and write the contraction.

20. _____

Family Tree: *would*   Think about how the *would* contractions are alike in spelling and meaning. Then add another *would* contraction to the tree.

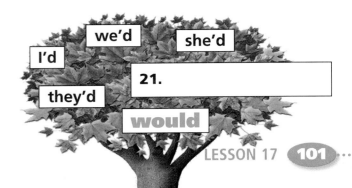

PECOS BILL

It _____ every day that a boy grows up with coyotes. But
1
then, Pecos Bill _____ an everyday fellow. When he just
2
was a baby, Bill drank mountain lion's milk. _____ think
3
that this would be hard to get! But for Bill's mother, it was a snap. Why,
_____ fight off an army single-handed!
4

Pecos Bill's father was one of the first to settle Texas, back when there
_____ many people around. But when people started
5
settling just fifty miles away, he knew it was time to go! "It's too crowded
around here," he said. "_____ pack up our things.
6
_____ going west."
7

The family piled into a wagon, with baby Bill in the back. As they
crossed the Pecos River, a large bump sent Bill flying out of the wagon! He
_____ call out
8
for help. Bill's family
_____ notice
9
he was gone until four weeks later. By that time
it was winter, and his family couldn't go back
to look for him. "Surely some people found
him," his dad said. "_____
10
take good care of him."

Bill was taken in by a pack of coyotes.
For ten happy years, he lived among

them. Because he _____ 11 seen any people, Bill was sure that he was one of the coyotes.

One day a cowboy came riding along and spotted Bill and his pet mountain lion fighting a bear. The cowboy talked to Bill. He promised that he _____ 12 hurt Bill, but Bill couldn't understand him. The cowboy taught Bill to speak. "You _____ 13 a coyote," he told Bill one day. "You're a boy."

"No, _____ 14 a coyote!" Bill said. "Listen. I can howl. Ah-ooooo!"

"That _____ 15 mean a thing!" said the cowboy. "Real coyotes have fur coats, _____ 16 they? Look at them. _____ 17 all got fur."

Bill glanced around. "I _____ 18 got any fur."

"You _____ 19 be here, _____ 20 for sure," said the cowboy. "Come home with me."

Bill said good-bye to his animal family. "I'll never forget you," he told them in coyote talk.

And Pecos Bill climbed upon his pet mountain lion and galloped off to a new life as the best cowboy the Texas prairie has ever seen.

that's
she'd
they've
weren't
doesn't
isn't
wouldn't
wasn't
aren't
we're
you'd
don't
I'm
hadn't
haven't
didn't
shouldn't
let's
couldn't
they'll

that's
she'd
they've
weren't
doesn't
isn't
wouldn't
wasn't
aren't
we're
you'd
don't
I'm
hadn't
haven't
didn't
shouldn't
let's
couldn't
they'll

Write to the Point

Write a brief tall tale about a character like Pecos Bill. What amazing powers does your character have? What does your character do with those amazing powers? Remember that tall tales stretch the truth, so let your imagination run free. Try to use spelling words from this lesson.

Use the strategies on page 7 when you are not sure how to spell a word.

Proofreading

Proofread this paragraph from a tall tale about Pecos Bill. Use proofreading marks to correct five spelling mistakes, three capitalization mistakes, and two punctuation mistakes.

Proofreading Marks
◯ spell correctly
≡ capitalize
⊙ add period

Pecos Bill Gets Hungry

One day Pecos Bill awoke from a long nap He'd been asleep for ten years! he was hungry, but he did'nt have anything to eat. He culdnn't lasso a bull, because he had lost his lasso. He'd have eaten snakes, but there werent' any

"I know what I'll do," bill said. "Im going to boil my boots. i will make boot stew!" And tha'ts exactly what he did.

Language Connection

Adjectives   An adjective describes a noun or pronoun by telling which one, what kind, or how many.

> Wouldn't you like a **tall** glass of **cold** lemonade?

> The **large glass** pitcher isn't in the cabinet.

Write each sentence below, correcting each misspelled word. Then circle the adjective in each sentence.

1. The video store did'nt have the movie I wanted.

_____

2. Wer'e starting a computer club at school.

_____

3. Becca dosen't want the lead role in the play.

_____

4. Yo'ud better pack your long raincoat.

_____

5. The guide said shed meet us by the iron gate.

_____

Challenge Yourself

Write the two words that make up each Challenge Word. Check the Spelling Dictionary to see if you are right. Then use separate paper to write sentences showing that you understand the meaning of each Challenge Word.

Challenge Words	
it'd	should've
must've	there're

6. **There're** some great storytellers in my family.   _____

7. My grandfather **should've** written his stories down to help me remember them.   _____

8. I **must've** been three years old when I first heard the story about the pet crocodile.   _____

9. The story isn't true, but **it'd** make a great movie.   _____

Lesson 18

Unit 3 Review
Lessons 13–17

Use the steps on page 6 to study words that are hard for you.

13
doctor
dollar
knock
problem
hospital
swallow
watch

Words with Short o

Write the spelling word that completes each analogy.

1. *Ten* is to *dime* as *one hundred* is to

   _____.

2. *Chef* is to *cook* as _____ is to *heal*.

3. *Answer* is to *question* as *solve* is to

   _____.

4. *Thermometer* is to *temperature* as

   _____ is to *time*.

5. *Lion* is to *cat* as _____ is to *bird*.

6. *Tap* is to *window* as _____ is to *door*.

7. *Teacher* is to *school* as *nurse* is to

   _____.

14
poem
ocean
clothes
throat
goes

Words with Long o

Write the spelling word that belongs in each group.

8. moves, travels, _____

9. outfits, garments, _____

10. verse, rhyme, _____

11. nose, mouth, _____

12. sea, river, _____

froze
knows
tomorrow
though

More Words with Long o

Write the spelling word for each clue.

13. If something got very cold, it did this.

_____

14. This word sounds like *crow*. _____

15. This word means the same as *understands*.

_____

16. This is the day after today. _____

jungle
suddenly
tough
trouble
does

Words with Short u

Write the spelling word for each definition.

17. without warning _____

18. strong _____

19. causes to happen _____

20. land with thick tropical plants

_____

21. difficulty _____

weren't
doesn't
we're
they've

Contractions

Write the spelling word that completes each sentence.

22. Marco _____ have enough money.

23. I know _____ going to be late.

24. I think _____ all gone home.

25. Why _____ we warned about the storm?

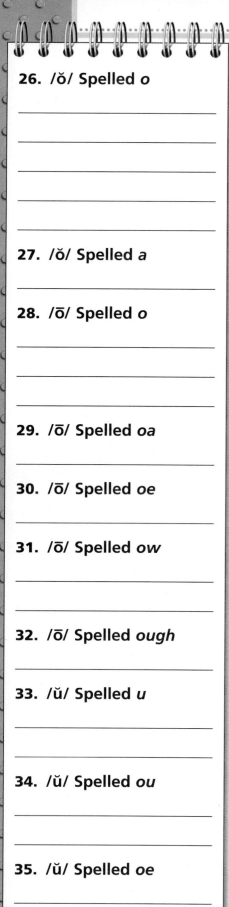

26. /ŏ/ Spelled o

_____
_____
_____
_____
_____

27. /ŏ/ Spelled a

_____

28. /ō/ Spelled o

_____
_____
_____

29. /ō/ Spelled oa

_____

30. /ō/ Spelled oe

_____

31. /ō/ Spelled ow

_____
_____

32. /ō/ Spelled ough

_____

33. /ŭ/ Spelled u

_____
_____

34. /ŭ/ Spelled ou

_____
_____

35. /ŭ/ Spelled oe

_____

Review Sort

watch	suddenly	hospital	though
poem	problem	knows	jungle
ocean	trouble	knock	goes
clothes	dollar	doctor	does
throat	tough	tomorrow	

26. Write the **five** /ŏ/ words with the _o_ pattern.
27. Write the **one** /ŏ/ word with the _a_ pattern.
28. Write the **three** /ō/ words with the _o_ pattern.
29. Write the **one** /ō/ word with the _oa_ pattern.
30. Write the **one** /ō/ word with the _oe_ pattern.
31. Write the **two** /ō/ words with the _ow_ pattern.
32. Write the **one** /ō/ word with the _ou_ pattern.
33. Write the **two** /ŭ/ words with the _u_ pattern.
34. Write the **two** /ŭ/ words with the _ou_ pattern.
35. Write the **one** /ŭ/ word with the _oe_ pattern.

These four words have been sorted into two groups. Explain how the words in each group are alike.

36. weren't   doesn't

_____
_____

37. she'd   you'd

_____
_____

Writer's Workshop

A Friendly Letter

Writing a letter is a nice way to keep in contact with someone. In a friendly letter, you can write in the same way that you speak. You might share some news about yourself or someone you know. You might also tell your feelings or thoughts about an event or subject. Here is part of a letter that Juanita wrote to her grandfather.

111 Leaf Circle
Carson City, NV 89701
December 9, 2002

Dear Grandpa,
    You won't believe this! Tabitha had four kittens. Two are gray, and two are striped. Mom won't let us keep any of them, but we've found good homes for them. I guess even one more cat would be too much for this apartment.

Prewriting   To write her letter, Juanita followed the steps in the writing process. After she decided to whom she would write, she created a list. In her list she wrote several things that she might include in her letter. Her list helped her decide what to tell her grandfather. Part of Juanita's list is shown here. Study what she wrote.

Letter to Grandpa

Tabitha's kittens
    four
    they are all asleep right now
    have to give away
    found good homes
two new friends
    like to skate
    in my class

It's Your Turn!

Write your own friendly letter. Your letter can be to a friend or family member whom you don't see very often. Before you write the letter, make a list like Juanita did. Choose things from the list that you think will interest your reader. Then follow the other steps in the writing process—writing, revising, proofreading, and publishing. Try to use spelling words from this lesson in your letter.

More Words with Short *u*

sponge

1. *o* Words

_____
_____
_____
_____
_____
_____
_____
_____
_____
_____
_____
_____
_____
_____
_____

2. *o*-consonant-*e* Words

_____
_____
_____

3. *oo* Word

_____

wonderful
discover
among
blood
front
other
brother
money
cover
month
monkey
done
sponge
nothing
above
stomach
once
become
another
won

Say and Listen

Say each spelling word. Listen for the short *u* sound.

Think and Sort

Look at the letters in each word. Think about how short *u* is spelled. Spell each word aloud.

Short *u* can be shown as /ŭ/. How many spelling patterns for /ŭ/ do you see?

1. Write the **sixteen** spelling words that have the *o* pattern.

2. Write the **three** spelling words that have the *o*-consonant-*e* pattern.

3. Write the **one** spelling word that has the *oo* pattern.

Use the steps on page 6 to study words that are hard for you.

Spelling Patterns

o	o-consonant-e	oo
front	become	blood

Antonyms   Write the spelling word that is an antonym of each word below.

1. below   _____
2. back   _____
3. unfinished   _____
4. lost   _____
5. horrible   _____
6. something   _____

Clues   Write the spelling word for each clue.

7. A girl is a sister, and a boy is this.   _____
8. Food is digested in this body part.   _____
9. This is one less than twice.   _____
10. This word means "to grow to be."   _____
11. Your heart pumps this through your body.   _____
12. This can soak up water.   _____
13. February is the shortest one.   _____
14. This word means "in the company of."   _____
15. This is a chimpanzee's cousin.   _____
16. This word completes the phrase
    "some ____ time."   _____
17. People use this to buy things.   _____
18. This means "one more."   _____
19. Do this to hide something.   _____

Word Story   A **prefix** is one or more letters added to the beginning of a base word. A prefix changes the meaning of the base word and makes a new word. One of the spelling words contains the prefix *dis-* and means "to find out." Write the word.

20. _____

Family Tree: *cover*   Think about how the *cover* words are alike in spelling and meaning. Then add another *cover* word to the tree.

covering

covers

uncover

21.

discover

cover

Use each spelling word once to complete the selection.

Monkeys

Millions of people visit the zoo each year. Large crowds always seem to gather in _____ of the _____ areas to watch
                         1   2
these funny, _____ animals at play.
                    3

The first monkeylike animals appeared millions of years ago. They were about the size of rats or mice and had warm _____. They
                                                                                    4
also had fur to _____ their body. These animals slept in the
                       5
daytime and lived high _____ the ground in trees. Over the
                               6
years, they grew to _____ the monkeys we see today.
                            7

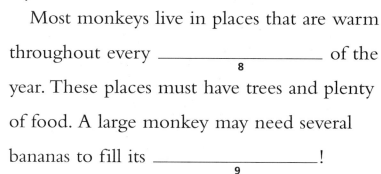

Most monkeys live in places that are warm throughout every _____ of the
                                                                         8
year. These places must have trees and plenty of food. A large monkey may need several bananas to fill its _____!
                                          9

Monkeys live in groups. Sometimes the group is divided into families. Each family contains a father, a mother, and even a sister and _____. Monkeys watch
              10
out for one _____. If one
                  11
of the animals should _____
                              12
danger, it will call out an alarm to the
_____ monkeys.
        13

howler monkey

capuchin monkey

wonderful
discover
among
blood
front
other
brother
money
cover
month
monkey
done
sponge
nothing
above
stomach
once
become
another
won

Monkeys are very smart. They take in information like a _____ soaking up water. When a monkey is
14
taught how to do a new task, the monkey repeats it with few
mistakes. Rhesus monkeys have even been used in space
flights! Some scientists have _____ awards for
15
work done with rhesus monkeys.

Even though monkeys are _____ the
16
best-loved animals in the world, the number of monkeys
grows smaller each year. One reason is that they are losing
their homes. Jungles that _____ were large
17
places for many monkeys to live are being cut down. Also,
some monkeys are killed for their fur, which is worth a lot
of _____. What is being _____
18   19
to stop the killing of monkeys? Laws to
protect them are often helpful.

Many people feel it would be wrong
to do _____ to save the
20
monkeys. What do you think?

rhesus monkey

wonderful
discover
among
blood
front
other
brother
money
cover
month
monkey
done
sponge
nothing
above
stomach
once
become
another
won

Write to the Point

What kinds of zoo animals have you seen? Have you observed animals such as elephants, giraffes, monkeys, or tigers? Choose an animal and write a paragraph about it. What does it look like? Where does it live? How does it spend its time? Try to use spelling words from this lesson.

> **Use the strategies on page 7 when you are not sure how to spell a word.**

Proofreading

Proofread the e-mail message below. Use proofreading marks to correct five spelling mistakes, three punctuation mistakes, and two unnecessary words.

Proofreading Marks
- ◯ spell correctly
- ⊙ add period
- ℒ take out

e-mail

| Address Book | Attachment | Check Spelling | Send | Save Draft | Cancel |

Alisha,

You won't believe what what my Uncle Dan does.

He works at the San Diego Zoo He wonce helped a

mother elephant bathe her baby. Anuther time he he

gave medicine to a giraffe with an upset stomick

He wants to becum an animal doctor I think he

has a wunderful job right now! Here is a picture

of him with one of the

elephants.

Reagan

Dictionary Skills

Accented Syllables   The dictionary entry for a word usually shows how the word is said. The way a word is said is called its pronunciation. An accent mark (′) tells which syllable is spoken with more stress, or force. In some dictionaries, dark type also indicates the accented syllable.

Study the accent marks in each pair of pronunciations below. Underline the pronunciation that shows the accent mark on the correct syllable. Then write the spelling word.

1. /mŭn ē′/   /**mŭn′** ē/   _____

2. /nŭth **ĭng′**/   /**nŭth′** ĭng/   _____

3. /**brŭth′** ər/   /brŭth ər′/   _____

Some words have two accented syllables. The strongest accent is the primary accent: (′). The weaker accent is the secondary accent: (′).

Look at this sound spelling: /**yĕs′** tər dā′/.

4. Write the syllable with the primary accent.   _____

5. Write the syllable with the secondary accent.   _____

6. Write the word correctly.   _____

Look at this sound spelling: /ăf′ tər **no͞on′**/

7. Write the syllable with the primary accent.   _____

8. Write the syllable with the secondary accent.   _____

9. Write the word correctly.   _____

☆Challenge Yourself

What do you think each Challenge Word means? Check the Spelling Dictionary to see if you are right. Then use separate paper to write sentences showing that you understand the meaning of each Challenge Word.

Challenge Words
loveliest
hover
wondrous
undiscovered

10. The beautiful tulips made Ping's garden the **loveliest** one in town.

11. We watched the hummingbird **hover** near the flowers.

12. Visiting the museum was a **wondrous** experience for Anita.

13. Although we know a great deal about oceans, many of their secrets remain **undiscovered**.

Words with /o͝o/

brook

1. *oo* **Words**

_____
_____
_____
_____
_____
_____
_____
_____

2. *u* **Words**

_____
_____
_____
_____
_____
_____

3. *ou* **Words**

_____
_____
_____
_____

4. *o* **Words**

_____
_____

wool
understood
cooked
should
stood
full
notebook
bush
brook
could
sugar
wooden
good-bye
pull
wolf
would
pudding
yours
during
woman

Say and Listen

Say each spelling word. Listen for the vowel sound you hear in *wool*.

Think and Sort

Look at the letters in each word. Think about how the vowel sound in *wool* is spelled. Spell each word aloud.

The vowel sound in *wool* can be shown as /o͝o/. How many spelling patterns for /o͝o/ do you see?

1. Write the **eight** spelling words that have the *oo* pattern.

2. Write the **six** spelling words that have the *u* pattern.

3. Write the **four** spelling words that have the *ou* pattern.

4. Write the **two** spelling words that have the *o* pattern.

Use the steps on page 6 to study words that are hard for you.

Spelling Patterns

oo	u	ou	o
wool	**full**	**could**	**wolf**

Spelling and Meaning

Synonyms   Write the spelling word that is a synonym for each word below.

1. tug _____

2. lady _____

3. while _____

4. stream _____

5. stuffed _____

6. shrub _____

If . . . Then   Write the spelling word that completes each sentence.

7. If you are cold, then put on a _____ sweater.

8. If you want dessert, then ask for cake or _____.

9. If you want to bake, then you may need _____ and flour.

10. If the meat is burnt, then it's been _____ too long.

11. If you need to write, then get a _____ and a pen.

12. If you hear a lone howl, then it might be a _____.

13. If it's not mine, then it may be _____.

14. If no one sat, then everyone _____.

15. If a bench is made from trees, then it's _____.

Rhymes   Use spelling words to complete the following poem.

16. I meant that I was able when I said, "I _____."

17. I meant that I really ought to when I said, "I _____."

18. I meant that I planned to do it when I said, "I _____."

19. I said it very clearly to be sure you _____!

Word Story   Long ago in England, the phrase "God be with you" was a common way of saying farewell. Over the years this phrase was shortened to "God be wy you." Even later it was shortened to "Godbwye." Write the spelling word it has become today.

20. _____

Family Tree: cooked   *Cooked* is a form of *cook*. Think about how the *cook* words are alike in spelling and meaning. Then add another *cook* word to the tree.

cooking

cooks

21. _____

cooker

uncooked

cook

Mrs. Novik's Place

When I was a child, my favorite season was autumn.

When the first cold autumn wind blew, my sister,

Caroline, and I would _____ on our _____
                              1   2

clothing and head for the woods. We _____ walk through
                                              3

miles of oak trees, sometimes spotting a deer hiding behind a

_____. Late in the afternoon, we would often hear a
          4

_____ howling in the distance.
          5

   A _____ bridge crossed a _____
                6   7

by Claney Mountain. Just past the bridge _____
                                                   8

a lonely cabin. It belonged to Mrs. Novik. Most people around

there thought that she was a strange old _____.
                                                    9

They said that children _____ stay away from her cabin.
                                   10

None of the adults _____ understand why Ma and Pa stood
                            11

up for Mrs. Novik, but Caroline and I _____, especially after
                                               12

one October day in 1892.

   Caroline and I brought Mrs. Novik some tasty _____
                                                          13

cookies that Ma had baked. Mrs. Novik served us some delicious

chocolate _____ that she had _____. When
                 14   15

Caroline and I were _____ of the wonderful treat, I read
                             16

Mrs. Novik a story I had written about her. "You are a fine writer,

Jonathan," she said when I finished. "I want to give you something." She

got up and came back with an old _____. "This is my diary,"
                                          17

she told me. "It tells the story of my life. Take it. It is now

_____ ."
   18

I sat by Mrs. Novik's fire all that afternoon, reading her diary.
From it I learned about her hard times _____ the
                                              19
Civil War. As I closed the book, a letter fell out:

Dear Mrs. Novik,

My husband is with us at last. Your food and care saved him. My family will never forget your kindness.

Mrs. Jonathan Walker

"Mrs. Jonathan Walker? That's Grandma!" I said. Then I
remembered Grandma's stories about the people of the
Underground Railroad and the lady who hid runaway slaves
during the war. Now I knew that the lady who hid Grandpa
was Mrs. Novik. Soon Caroline and I told Mrs. Novik

_____ and headed home. I couldn't wait
        20
to tell Ma and Pa what I had learned.

The cabin is gone now, and so is that old
bridge. But sometimes even now, I hike
out to Claney Mountain in the autumn.
I think about Mrs. Novik and the great
kindness she showed to my family.

wool
understood
cooked
should
stood
full
notebook
bush
brook
could
sugar
wooden
good-bye
pull
wolf
would
pudding
yours
during
woman

wool
understood
cooked
should
stood
full
notebook
bush
brook
could
sugar
wooden
good-bye
pull
wolf
would
pudding
yours
during
woman

Write to the Point

Mrs. Novik is an important person to Jonathan and his family. Is there an older person in your family or in your neighborhood who is interesting or important to you? Write a paragraph that describes this person. Include the details that make this person special. Try to use spelling words from this lesson.

Use the strategies on page 7 when you are not sure how to spell a word.

Proofreading

Proofread the book review paragraph below. Use proofreading marks to correct five spelling mistakes, three capitalization mistakes, and two punctuation mistakes.

Proofreading Marks
◯ spell correctly
≡ capitalize
⊙ add period

A Look Backward

Buggies and Butter Churns is Caroline lee's book about her life as a young womon durring the late 1800s. on summer days she fished in a bruk on the farm. In the fall she made maple suger from sap. In the spring she spun yarn from wull. The title comes from Lee's favorite and least favorite things She loved driving a buggy but hated churning butter. lee's book gives readers an interesting look at life in a simpler time

Language Connection

Capitalization   When the words *mother, father, mom,* and *dad* are used in place of names, they begin with a capital letter. When words such as *aunt, uncle,* and *doctor* are used as titles before a name, they begin with a capital letter. These words do not begin with a capital letter when they follow *a, an, the,* or a possessive word such as *my, your,* or *Bob's.*

> My uncle took **M**om and **A**unt **R**osa to the doctor's office.

The following sentences have errors in capitalization and spelling. Write each sentence correctly.

1. my Father cood not fix our broken lawnmower.

   _____

2. uncle frank and dad stoud in line for baseball tickets.

   _____

3. Danny's Father said gud-bye to dr. dominguez.

   _____

4. We took a picture of mom and dad near the wuden bridge.

   _____

5. My Aunt asked uncle Mike to share his recipe for bread puding.

   _____

Challenge Yourself

Write the Challenge Word for each clue. Check the Spelling Dictionary to see if you are right. Then use separate paper to write sentences showing that you understand the meaning of each Challenge Word.

Challenge Words
bookstore
misunderstood
rural
swoosh

6. This word describes fields of farms and open land.

   _____

7. This is a rushing and swirling sound.   _____

8. If writers do not write clearly, they might be this.   _____

9. This building always has many stories.   _____

Words with /o͞o/ or /yo͞o/

cougar

Word List

goose
beautiful
cougar
route
balloon
too
soup
knew
group
two
grew
through
new
cartoon
truly
fruit
loose
shoot
truth
choose

Say and Listen

Say each spelling word. Listen for the vowel sound you hear in *goose* and *beautiful*.

Think and Sort

The vowel sound in *goose* and *beautiful* can be shown as /o͞o/. In *beautiful* and some other /o͞o/ words, a *y* is pronounced before the /o͞o/.

Look at the letters in each word. Think about how /o͞o/ or /yo͞o/ is spelled. Spell each word aloud.

1. Write the **seven** spelling words that have the *oo* pattern.

2. Write the **three** spelling words that have the *ew* pattern.

3. Write the **two** spelling words that have the *u* pattern.

4. Write the **five** spelling words that have the *ou* pattern.

5. Write the **three** spelling words that have the *ui, o,* or *eau* pattern.

Use the steps on page 6 to study words that are hard for you.

1. *oo* Words

_____
_____
_____
_____
_____
_____
_____

2. *ew* Words

_____
_____
_____

3. *u* Words

_____
_____

4. *ou* Words

_____
_____
_____
_____
_____

5. *ui, o, eau* Words

_____
_____
_____

Spelling Patterns

oo	ew	u	ou	ui	o	eau
goose	new	truth	group	fruit	two	beautiful

Spelling and Meaning

Homophones   Write the spelling word that is a homophone of each word below.

1. chute   _____
2. knew   _____
3. root   _____
4. threw   _____
5. two   _____

Analogies   Write the spelling word that completes each analogy.

6. *Throw* is to *threw* as *know* is to _____.
7. *One* is to _____ as *A* is to *B*.
8. *Yes* is to *no* as *ugly* is to _____.
9. *Day* is to *night* as _____ is to *lie*.
10. *Bird* is to *flock* as *member* is to _____.
11. *Dirt* is to *flowerpot* as *air* is to _____.
12. *Light* is to *dark* as *tight* is to _____.
13. *Rabbit* is to *fur* as _____ is to *feather*.
14. *Apple* is to _____ as *spinach* is to *vegetable*.
15. *Afraid* is to *frightened* as *really* is to _____.
16. *Fork* is to *spaghetti* as *spoon* is to _____.
17. *Painter* is to *painting* as *cartoonist* is to _____.
18. *Smile* is to *grin* as _____ is to *pick*.
19. *Fly* is to *flew* as *grow* is to _____.

Word Story   One of the spelling words names an animal that is the same color as a deer. The word comes from the Tupi Indian word *suasuarana*. *Suasuarana* meant "false deer." The name became *couguar* in French. Write the word.

20. _____

Family Tree: *knew*   *Knew* is a form of *know*. Think about how the *know* words are alike in spelling and meaning. Then add another *know* word to the tree.

knowledge

knows

known

21.

knew

know

The Life of a Snow Goose

Have you ever seen a _____ of snow geese flying across
the sky? Like a well-trained dancer, each _____ keeps its
place in the flock while flying. The flock often flies in the shape of a V.
Now that is a _____ sight!

In the spring, snow geese fly north to their nesting grounds. When they
arrive, they_____ nesting places. After a male and female
choose a spot, the _____ of them fight off any goose that
comes _____ close. Then the mother lays her eggs. The
parents scare away enemies, such as the Arctic fox. When defending its nest,
a snow goose can be as fierce as a snarling _____.

After the eggs hatch, the parents teach the babies to find food and
to fly. Snow geese keep their little ones in a group. They do not let them
run _____. At night the whole family sleeps together.
Snow geese are _____ good parents!

In the fall the snow geese fly south. When they get hungry, they land
in a field. They eat seeds, tender green plants, and _____
such as cranberries.

For hundreds of years, flocks of geese followed the same

_____ every year. Somehow they always
          11

_____ how to find the same path. They could fly
          12

through fog as thick as pea _____ without losing
              13

their way! Flocks often take a _____ route today.
                 14

This route passes _____ areas where there are
          15

grain farms. The geese eat the grains to fatten up for the winter.

    It is hard for the grain farmers to watch the crops that they

_____ be eaten by geese. That is why they try to
          16

scare the geese away. Some farmers tie a brightly colored

helium _____ to each fence post. Other farmers
             17

_____ firecrackers into the air.
          18

    The _____ on this page is a joke, but it tells
            19

the _____ about snow geese. They do not like
        20

freezing weather, so they spend the winter in a warm place.

At winter's end, they return to their nesting grounds to start

new families.

Spelling and Writing

goose
beautiful
cougar
route
balloon
too
soup
knew
group
two
grew
through
new
cartoon
truly
fruit
loose
shoot
truth
choose

Write to the Point

As you walk through your neighborhood, what kinds of birds do you see? Write a paragraph that tells about one of these birds. Find out interesting facts to include. Try to use some of the spelling words from this lesson in your writing.

Use the strategies on page 7 when you are not sure how to spell a word.

Proofreading

Proofread the paragraph below. Use proofreading marks to correct five spelling mistakes, three capitalization mistakes, and two punctuation mistakes.

Proofreading Marks
◯ spell correctly
≡ capitalize
⊙ add period

The Canada Goose

the name of one kind of gouse might lead you to think that it lives only in canada. The trooth is that Canada geese live throughout North America Many of these beootiful birds live close to people. Some live in parks Others live in ponds close to neighborhoods. sometimes a groop of Canada geese chooses to make its home on a noo golf course!

Dictionary Skills

Homophones   Words that sound the same but have different spellings and meanings are called homophones. If a word is a homophone, some dictionaries list the other homophones at the end of the entry.

> **through** (thro͞o) *prep.* **1.** In one side and out the opposite side of: *through the tunnel.* **2.** Among; in the midst of: *a road through the woods. These sound alike:* **through, threw.**

Use the homophones in the boxes at right to answer the questions and complete the sentences below. Use the Spelling Dictionary if you need to.

1. Which word is the opposite of *old*? _____

2. Which word is the past tense of *know*? _____

3. Which word names a number? _____

4. Which word means "also"? _____

5. Even though the quarterback was _____,
   he _____ all the plays.

6. When the other team made _____ points,
   the star player on our team scored points, _____.

Challenge Yourself

Use the Spelling Dictionary to answer the questions. Then use separate paper to write sentences showing that you understand the meaning of each Challenge Word.

Challenge Words	
accuse	boost
contribute	coupon

7. Would a small child need a **boost** to climb onto a horse? _____

8. Do you pay more money for an item at the grocery store when you use a **coupon**? _____

9. If you **accuse** someone of stealing, are you saying he or she did something wrong? _____

10. Do people **contribute** cans and boxes of food to help feed others?

    _____

Lesson 22 Words with /ou/

tower

1. *ou* Words

_____
_____
_____
_____
_____
_____
_____
_____
_____
_____

2. *ow* Words

_____
_____
_____
_____
_____
_____
_____
_____
_____
_____

loud
counter
somehow
hours
powerful
sour
crowd
growl
cloud
towel
ours
south
crowded
mouth
vowel
shower
crown
tower
noun
proud

Say and Listen

Say each spelling word. Listen for the vowel sound you hear in *loud*.

Think and Sort

Look at the letters in each word. Think about how the vowel sound in *loud* is spelled. Spell each word aloud.

The vowel sound in *loud* can be shown as /ou/. How many spelling patterns for /ou/ do you see?

1. Write the **ten** spelling words that have the *ou* pattern.

2. Write the **ten** spelling words that have the *ow* pattern.

Use the steps on page 6 to study words that are hard for you.

Spelling Patterns

ou	ow
loud	crown

Spelling and Meaning

Classifying   Write the spelling word that belongs in each group.

1. robe, throne, _____
2. seconds, minutes, _____
3. eye, nose, _____
4. group, bunch, _____
5. sweet, salty, _____
6. noisy, booming, _____
7. drizzle, sprinkle, _____
8. bark, snarl, _____
9. east, north, _____
10. mighty, strong, _____
11. yours, theirs, _____
12. full, packed, _____

Partner Words   Complete each sentence by writing the spelling word that goes with the underlined word.

13. Do you want to sit in a <u>booth</u> or at the _____?
14. <u>Someone</u> somewhere must rescue the princess _____.
15. The castle had a _____ and a <u>moat</u>.
16. I'll get you a _____ and a <u>washcloth</u>.
17. <u>Rain</u> will soon fall from that dark _____.
18. Jamal was <u>pleased</u> with and _____ of his sister's work.
19. You can choose a _____ or a <u>consonant</u>.

Word Story   One of the spelling words names a part of speech. It comes from the Latin word *nomen,* meaning "name." Write the word.

20. _____

Family Tree: *powerful*   *Powerful* is a form of *power*. Think about how the *power* words are alike in spelling and meaning. Then add another *power* word to the tree.

- powered
- powerless
- powers
- powerful
- 21.
- power

Use each spelling word once to complete the selection.

An Ancient Code

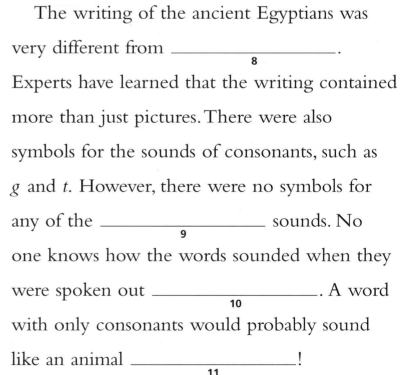

Did you know that writing came from art? People had been drawing pictures for thousands of years. As time passed, they _____ got the

1

idea of using pictures to stand for words. In picture writing, each picture stands for a verb or a _____. For example, a picture of a

2

_____ might stand for *king*. A _____ of

3   4

raindrops falling from a _____ might stand for *rain*. A

5

_____ or lips might be used for *talk* or *say*. Early Egyptians

6

used picture writing. They drew each picture very carefully. It took them

many _____ to write a message.

7

The writing of the ancient Egyptians was very different from _____.

8

Experts have learned that the writing contained more than just pictures. There were also symbols for the sounds of consonants, such as *g* and *t*. However, there were no symbols for any of the _____ sounds. No

9

one knows how the words sounded when they were spoken out _____. A word

10

with only consonants would probably sound like an animal _____!

11

Picture writing has been found in both the north and the

_____ of Egypt. The writings show how
₁₂

_____ Egyptians were of their rulers and their
₁₃

gods. Writing covered the walls of temples. Tales of strong and

_____ rulers were carved on obelisks. An
₁₄

obelisk is a tall, thin _____.
₁₅

Picture writing has also been found on mummies and

treasures in many Egyptian tombs. As workers wrapped a

mummy, they hid picture messages. First, workers laid the

body on a long wooden table or _____ to wash
₁₆

it. Then, they used a _____ to rub on perfumed
₁₇

oil. That kept the body from smelling _____.
₁₈

Last, they wrapped the body in cloth strips. Between the layers

of cloth, they tucked notes in picture writing. The notes

warned away bad spirits. Then a large _____ of
₁₉

mourners carried the body to the tomb. Others carried food,

clothing, and jewels. They buried these things with their loved

one. A tomb could be very _____!
₂₀

After modern scientists found the tombs, they spent years

studying the picture writing there. The writing reveals much

about ancient Egyptian life. As scientists have learned to decode

the writing, they have unlocked a door to the past.

loud
counter
somehow
hours
powerful
sour
crowd
growl
cloud
towel
ours
south
crowded
mouth
vowel
shower
crown
tower
noun
proud

water   loaf   owl   foot   chick   door bolt   snake   folded cloth

loud
counter
somehow
hours
powerful
sour
crowd
growl
cloud
towel
ours
south
crowded
mouth
vowel
shower
crown
tower
noun
proud

Write to the Point

You have learned some interesting facts about writing. Now you can do some interesting writing of your own. First, write a sentence or message you'd like to send, using spelling words from this lesson. Then decide what kind of code to use. You can even make one up. For example, you can use pictures to stand for letters or words. You can have one letter of the alphabet stand for the one before it. Or you can write backwards! Last, write your message in code.

Use the strategies on page 7 when you are not sure how to spell a word.

Proofreading

Proofread the journal entry below. Use proofreading marks to correct five spelling mistakes, three capitalization mistakes, and two missing words.

Proofreading Marks

◯ spell correctly
≡ capitalize
∧ add

october 21

I think writing amazing. a letter can stand

for a consonant or vowl. A group of letters

can form a word. The word might be a

nown. At other times it might be a verb.

When words put together in the right way,

they somhow make ideas come alive. Ideas

are powrful. i think that anyone would be

prowd to be a writer.

Language Connection

Quotation Marks   Use quotation marks around the exact words of a speaker. Capitalize the first word in the quotation.

> Chester asked, "What letter of the alphabet do you drink?"
> "I drink tea," Lester replied.

Write the following sentences. Use quotation marks and capital letters where needed. Spell the misspelled words correctly.

1. Julie said, a big croud always comes to see our team play.

_____

_____

2. they practice for three howrs each day, said Brian.

_____

_____

3. even when they're behind, they don't throw in the towle, said Chris.

_____

_____

4. let's give them a lowd cheer! shouted Ben.

_____

_____

Challenge Yourself

Write the Challenge Word for each clue. Check the Spelling Dictionary to see if you are right. Then use separate paper to write sentences showing that you understand the meaning of each Challenge Word.

Challenge Words	
drowsy	counselor
encounter	blouse

5. This is a person you go to for advice. _____

6. Seeing a friend at a store and stopping to say hello is an example of this. _____

7. A girl wears this piece of clothing with pants or a skirt.

_____

8. It's how you feel early in the morning after staying up too late.

_____

Words with -ed or -ing

swimming

Spelling Words

swimming
asked
hoping
changed
pleased
beginning
caused
traded
closing
invited
tasted
jogging
studied
copied
dried
saving
cried
trying
carrying
writing

1. No Change to Base Word

_____
_____
_____

2. Final e Dropped

_____
_____
_____
_____
_____
_____
_____
_____
_____
_____

3. Final Consonant Doubled

_____
_____
_____

4. Final y Changed to i

_____
_____
_____
_____

Say and Listen

Say the spelling words. Listen for the -ed and -ing endings.

Think and Sort

A word from which other words are formed is called a **base word**. The spelling of some base words changes when -ed or -ing is added.

Look at the base word and the ending in each spelling word. Spell each word aloud.

1. Write the **three** spelling words that have no change to the base word.

2. Write the **ten** spelling words formed by dropping the final e before -ed or -ing is added.

3. Write the **three** spelling words formed by doubling the final consonant before -ing is added.

4. Write the **four** spelling words formed by changing the final y to i before -ed is added.

Use the steps on page 6 to study words that are hard for you.

Spelling Patterns

No Change to Base Word	Final e Dropped	Final Consonant Doubled	Final y Changed to i
ask**ed**	hop**ing**	swi**mming**	stud**ied**

Spelling and Meaning

Making Connections   Write the spelling word that goes with each person.

1. a mail carrier _____
2. a lifeguard _____
3. a runner _____
4. a cook _____
5. an author _____
6. a baby _____
7. a student _____

If . . . Then   Write the spelling word that completes each sentence.

8. If Ramon exchanged baseball cards, then he _____ them.
9. If Carlos is putting money in a bank, then he's _____ it.
10. If Amad wishes for a bicycle, then he's _____ for one.
11. If Mr. Bina is shutting the door, then he's _____ it.
12. If Tyler begged for help, then he _____ for it.
13. If Dad liked the work, then he was _____ with it.
14. If Sarah imitated the star's hairdo, then she _____ it.
15. If Troy asked his friends to a party, then he _____ them.
16. If the sun is coming up, then it is _____ to be seen.
17. If Sam wiped away his tears, then he _____ them.
18. If Lamont is not the same, then he has _____.
19. If heavy rain loosened the mud, then it _____ a mud slide.

Word Story   One of the spelling words comes from the Old French word *trier*. *Trier* meant "to pick out." The spelling word has several meanings — "to sample," "to test," or "to attempt." Write the *-ing* form of this word.

20. _____

Family Tree: *pleased*   *Pleased* is a form of *please*. Think about how the *please* words are alike in spelling and meaning. Then add another *please* word to the tree.

- displeased
- pleased
- pleasure
- 21.
- pleasant
- pleases
- **please**

J.J. Returns to the Sea

A mother whale was on her way south when something unexpected happened. The baby she was _____ was born early! The baby whale, or calf,
₁

had trouble _____ in the cold ocean water. The calf lost her way.
₂

One day the calf swam near a California beach. People who were walking

and _____ along the shore saw that the young whale was
₃

in trouble. They _____ others to help. Soon police and animal
₄

experts were _____ to get the baby to shore. Finally, they got
₅

the whale onto a truck. Then they took her to a marine park. This move

_____ everyone.
₆

Caretakers at the park named the baby whale J.J. The animal doctors there

_____ J.J. The young whale was constantly _____
₇ ₈

her eyes. She could not hold herself steady. What had _____ these
₉

problems? J.J. was only one week old and hadn't eaten in days!

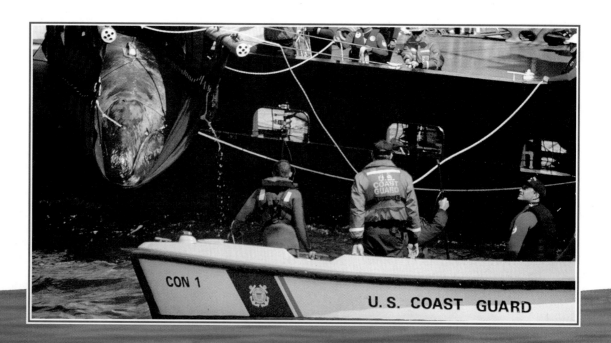

The doctors mixed cream, fish, and water for her. They hoped the

mix _____ like the milk J. J. was used to. In the
         10

_____, J. J.'s caretakers poured her food down a tube
         11

to her stomach. Soon, however, the calf could drink for herself.

Many people were interested in J. J.'s recovery. Caretakers began

_____ messages on a special Web site. They wanted
         12

to let J. J.'s fans know how she was doing.

During J. J.'s first month at the park, she _____
                                                    13

a lot. J. J. gained 900 pounds! Caretakers _____
                                                  14

her small pool for a roomier one. _____ that J. J.
                                          15

would learn to communicate, they then began playing whale songs

for her. J. J. listened to the recordings and _____
                                                      16

the sounds she heard.

Soon it was time for J. J. to go back to the sea. Her caretakers

were _____ to ride with J. J. in the truck. They
          17

sprayed J. J. with water often to keep her skin from becoming

_____ out.
         18

At last J. J. was lowered into the sea. As her caretakers said

good-bye, some _____. They had played a big part
                      19

in _____ J. J.'s life and would miss her. Everyone
       20

knew, however, that J. J. was finally back where she belonged!

swimming
asked
hoping
changed
pleased
beginning
caused
traded
closing
invited
tasted
jogging
studied
copied
dried
saving
cried
trying
carrying
writing

Spelling and Writing

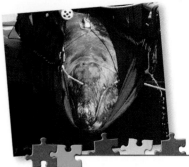

Write to the Point

Have you ever had an opportunity to rescue someone's pet or an animal living in the wild? Why did the animal need help? What did you do to help? What was the outcome? Write a paragraph that answers these questions. Try to use spelling words from this lesson.

Use the strategies on page 7 when you are not sure how to spell a word.

Proofreading

Proofread the magazine article below. Use proofreading marks to correct five spelling mistakes, three capitalization mistakes, and two unnecessary words.

Proofreading Marks
◯ spell correctly
≡ capitalize
ℓ take out

Spelling words list:

swimming
asked
hoping
changed
pleased
beginning
caused
traded
closing
invited
tasted
jogging
studied
copied
dried
saving
cried
trying
carrying
writing

Rescue Ray

by Alexa Brown

Early one morning Ray Joseph was

joging down Oak street. Suddenly

he heard a crying sound high in a tree. Ray wondered what

could could make such a sound. Then he saw a fluffy gray kitten.

Ray studied the tree. How would he get up there? meanwhile

the kitten cryed louder and louder.

Saveing the kitten was not as hard as Ray thought. Soon a

little girl ran up to him. "That's my theo," she said. Ray was

pleazed that he had had been able to help.

Language Connection

Predicates   The predicate of a sentence tells what the subject of the sentence is or does.

> The little girl **skipped down the street.**

Write the predicate in each sentence.

1. My cousin Jenny invited me to come to her house last summer.

_____

2. Jenny and I swam in the pool each day.

_____

3. Jenny's brothers and I traded our favorite mystery stories.

_____

A predicate often contains a main verb and a helping verb. In the sentence below, *jogging* is the main verb. *Are* is the helping verb. The predicate begins with the helping verb.

> My friends **are jogging down the sidewalk.**

Write the predicate in each sentence. Circle the helping verb.

4. My famous grandmother is writing a book.   _____

5. Many people are reading her other books.   _____

Challenge Yourself

What do you think each Challenge Word means? Check the Spelling Dictionary to see if you are right. Then use separate paper to write sentences showing that you understand the meaning of each Challenge Word.

Challenge Words

hustled
importing
overlapping
fortified

6. Because I overslept, I **hustled** to meet the school bus on time.

7. The United States is **importing** oil from several countries.

8. Be sure the edges of the tent are **overlapping** so that rain can't get in.

9. During the flood, we **fortified** the banks of the river with sandbags.

Unit 4 Review
Lessons 19–23

Use the steps on page 6 to study words that are hard for you.

 19

discover
stomach
wonderful
once
blood

More Words with Short *u*

Write the spelling word that belongs in each group.

1. realize, notice, _____

2. sweat, tears, _____

3. fantastic, splendid, _____

4. lung, kidney, _____

5. never, twice, _____

 20

understood
during
sugar
should
woman

Words with /o͞o/

Write the spelling word that completes each analogy.

6. *Sour* is to *lemon* as *sweet* is to

_____.

7. *Shall* is to _____ as *will* is to *would*.

8. *Run* is to *ran* as *understand* is to

_____.

9. *Boy* is to *man* as *girl* is to

_____.

10. *After* is to *following* as *throughout*
is to _____.

 21

loose
truly
knew
through
fruit
two
beautiful

Words with /o͞o/ or /yo͞o/

Write the spelling word for each definition.

11. in one side and out the other _____

12. lovely to look at or listen to _____

13. the number between one and three _____

14. not tight _____

15. really, honestly _____

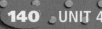

16. the juicy, seed-bearing part of
a plant _____

17. had knowledge of _____

Words with /ou/

22 loud
ours
crowd

Write the spelling word for each clue.

18. This develops when many people gather together.

_____

19. People cover their ears because a noise is this.

_____

20. If something belongs to us, it is this. _____

Words with -ed or -ing

23 asked
trying
hoping
beginning
copied

Write the spelling word that completes each sentence.

21. "Can you write a better ending for your story?"
_____ Elsa's teacher.

22. "I have been _____ to do that,"
replied Elsa.

23. "I will read the story again
from the _____."

24. Elsa _____ the
story for her classmates to read.

25. Everyone was _____
that the ending was happy.

26. /ŭ/ with *o* Words

_____

_____

_____

27. /ŭ/ with *oo* Word

_____

28. /o͝o/ Words

_____

_____

_____

_____

_____

29. /o͞o/ Words

_____

_____

_____

_____

_____

_____

30. /yo͞o/ Word

_____

31. /ou/ with *ou* Words

_____

_____

32. /ou/ with *ow* Word

_____

Review Sort

through   understood   sugar   two
stomach   wonderful   truly   ours
blood   beautiful   discover   fruit
loud   loose   knew   should
during   once   woman   crowd

26. Write the **four** /ŭ/ words with the *o* pattern.

27. Write the **one** /ŭ/ word with the *oo* pattern.

28. Write the **five** /o͝o/ words. Circle the letter or letters that spell /o͝o/ in each word.

29. Write the **six** /o͞o/ words. Circle the letter or letters that spell /o͞o/ in each word.

30. Write **one** /yo͞o/ word. Circle the letters that spell /yo͞o/ in the word.

31. Write the **two** /ou/ words with the *ou* pattern.

32. Write the **one** /ou/ word with the *ow* pattern.

These five words have been sorted into two groups. Explain how the words in each group are alike and how they are different.

33. hoping   beginning   trying

_____

_____

_____

34. copied   asked

_____

_____

_____

Writer's Workshop

A Description

A description tells about a person, place, or thing. In a description, writers use details that appeal to a reader's senses of sight, hearing, smell, touch, and taste. Here is part of Carlotta's description of a birthday cake.

Prewriting   To write her description, Carlotta followed the steps in the writing process. After she decided on a topic, she completed a senses web. In the web she listed details that appealed to the senses. The web helped Carlotta decide which details to include in her description. Part of Carlotta's senses web is shown here. Study what Carlotta did.

A Cake to Remember

The cake was covered with fluffy white frosting and topped with roses made of pink, yellow, and green frosting. A white candle stood in each rose. Beneath the frosting stood two layers of dark cake with a sticky brown filling between them. The filling smelled like chocolate and had crunchy nuts and chewy bits of coconut in it.

Sight
fluffy white frosting
pink, yellow, green roses
white candles
dark cake

birthday cake

It's Your Turn!

Write your own description. It can be about a place, a person, or anything you can picture clearly in your mind. After you have decided on your topic, make a senses web. Then follow the other steps in the writing process—writing, revising, proofreading, and publishing. Try to use spelling words from this lesson in your description.

Lesson 25 Words with /oi/

soil

1. *oy* Words

_____
_____
_____
_____
_____
_____
_____
_____
_____

2. *oi* Words

_____
_____
_____
_____
_____
_____
_____
_____
_____
_____
_____

coin
moisture
enjoy
spoil
destroy
employ
point
employer
loyal
royal
poison
soil
join
voyage
loyalty
avoid
voice
noise
soybean
choice

Say and Listen

Say each spelling word. Listen for the vowel sound you hear in *coin.*

Think and Sort

Look at the letters in each word. Think about how the vowel sound in *coin* is spelled. Spell each word aloud.

The vowel sound in *coin* can be shown as /oi/. How many spelling patterns for /oi/ do you see?

1. Write the **nine** spelling words that have the *oy* pattern.

2. Write the **eleven** spelling words that have the *oi* pattern.

Use the steps on page 6 to study words that are hard for you.

Spelling Patterns

oy	oi
enjoy	coin

Spelling and Meaning

Clues Write the spelling word for each clue.

1. A ship can take you on this. _____
2. This is very harmful to living things. _____
3. You can dig in this. _____
4. Dogs are this to their masters. _____
5. When you can decide between two things, you have this. _____
6. You put this in a parking meter. _____
7. The end of an arrow has this. _____
8. An opera singer uses this. _____
9. People work for this person. _____
10. This plant has nutritious seeds. _____
11. Good friends share this with each other. _____
12. Water adds this to the air. _____

Antonyms Complete each sentence by writing the spelling word that is an antonym of the underlined word.

13. They had to _____ the old house and build a new one.
14. We can separate or _____ these two wires.
15. Will the rain improve or _____ the crops?
16. Do you dislike your dancing lessons or _____ them?
17. Hector needs silence in order to study, not _____.
18. Will the store fire its workers and _____ new ones?
19. I will meet Laura at the store early and _____ the crowd.

Word Story Three English words mean "fit for a king." *Kingly* is from the Old English word *king. Regal* comes from the Latin word *rex.* One of the spelling words comes from the French word *roi.* Write the word.

20. _____

Family Tree: *point* Think about how the *point* words are alike in spelling and meaning. Then add another *point* word to the tree.

points

pointer

pointed

21.

pointless

point

Use each spelling word once to complete the selection.

Treasure from China

During the 1200s and 1300s, many travelers visited China. One of them was the explorer Marco Polo. After a very long _____ by sea and land, Polo arrived in China in 1274.

There he earned the trust of the ruler, Kublai Khan. Polo worked in China's government and was _____ to Kublai Khan. In return Khan rewarded Polo's service and _____ with many gifts. In 1292 Marco Polo thanked his generous _____ and returned to Italy with spices, jade, silk, and stories.

Polo told other people about the many treasures he saw in China. In a _____ loud and clear, he described the beauty and loud _____ of fireworks. He told how paper money was used instead of a single gold or silver _____. But neither Polo nor any of the other visitors to China talked about the small green bean that grew in China's fields—the _____. That small green bean became a great world treasure.

Soybeans did not reach Europe until the 1700s. They were grown in special gardens in France. They were even grown in the English king's _____ gardens. Soon the Chinese beans were brought to North America. At that _____ an important industry began.

Scientists in the United States studied about 10,000 kinds of soybeans. Farmers could decide which one was the best

_____ 11 for their part of the country. Some kinds needed lots of rain. Others needed less _____ 12.

Soybeans could grow in almost any kind of dirt. They did best, however, in rich, well-drained _____ 13. The plants were easy to keep healthy, too. A plant disease would almost never _____ 14 the whole crop. Scientists later developed soybean plants that did not attract insects. In fact, bugs would _____ 15 the new plants. Since most bugs stayed away, farmers could use less _____ 16.

Today soybean farms _____ 17 thousands of workers. Soybeans are used to make everything from paint to pet food. They are used in many foods that people eat and _____ 18 every day, such as cereal and ice cream.

As countries _____ 19 together to fight world hunger, soybeans are their best weapon. Soybeans have more protein than meat. They don't _____ 20 or rot. Soybeans cost less than meat, too! Of all the treasures China has given the world, the soybean may just be the most important.

coin
moisture
enjoy
spoil
destroy
employ
point
employer
loyal
royal
poison
soil
join
voyage
loyalty
avoid
voice
noise
soybean
choice

Spelling and Writing

coin
moisture
enjoy
spoil
destroy
employ
point
employer
loyal
royal
poison
soil
join
voyage
loyalty
avoid
voice
noise
soybean
choice

Write to the Point

The soybean is used to make many foods that are good for people. What healthful foods do you like most? Choose one and write an advertisement for it. Include information about where the food grows, why it is good for people, and how it tastes. Try to use spelling words from this lesson.

Use the strategies on page 7 when you are not sure how to spell a word.

Proofreading

Proofread the letter below. Use proofreading marks to correct five spelling mistakes, three punctuation mistakes, and two unnecessary words.

Proofreading Marks
◯ spell correctly
⊙ add period
ᵔ take out

2840 Red Hill Avenue

Avon, OH 44011

July 17, 2003

Dear Trina,

Do you enjoi eating tomatoes? We have a great crop this

this year Too much rain can can spoyl the crop Too little rain

can destroi it, too This summer's rains added just enough

moischer to the soyle. I hope to see you soon!

Your friend,

Maria

Dictionary Skills

Parts of Speech   Some words can be used as more than one part of speech. The parts of speech include noun (*n.*), verb (*v.*), adjective (*adj.*), adverb (*adv.*), and preposition (*prep.*). Sometimes the parts of speech are listed within one dictionary entry.

> **poi·son** (poi′ zən) *n.* Any substance dangerous to life and health: *Bottles containing poison are clearly marked.* —*v.* **poi·soned, poi·son·ing.** To kill or harm with poison

At other times they are listed in two dictionary entries.

> **soil¹** (soil) *n.* The top layer of the earth's surface in which seeds are planted; dirt.

> **soil²** (soil) *v.* **soiled, soil·ing.** To make or become dirty: *Jarrell soiled his white T-shirt.*

Use *soil* and *poison* to complete the sentences below. Then write *noun* or *verb* after each to tell how it is used in the sentence.

1. Grandma planted flower seeds in the _____.
   _____

2. Some everyday cleaners can _____ your plants.
   _____

3. Bottles containing _____ should be clearly marked.
   _____

4. Don't _____ your clothes by digging in that dirt!
   _____

Challenge Yourself

Write the Challenge Word for each clue. Check the Spelling Dictionary to see if you are right. Then use separate paper to write sentences showing that you understand the meaning of each Challenge Word.

Challenge Words	
appoint	poise
pointless	toil

5. People who have this are calm under pressure.   _____

6. To pull weeds all day in the hot sun is to do this.   _____

7. This word tells what it is like to try to teach a fish to talk.   _____

8. This is one way a teacher can get a helper.   _____

Lesson 26

Words with /ô/

autumn

Spelling Words List

pause
already
brought
strong
taught
caught
cause
because
wrong
coffee
bought
thought
author
applaud
autumn
daughter
gone
offer
often
office

Say and Listen

Say each spelling word. Listen for the vowel sound you hear in *pause.*

Think and Sort

Look at the letters in each word. Think about how the vowel sound in *pause* is spelled. Spell each word aloud.

The vowel sound in *pause* can be shown as /ô/. How many spelling patterns for /ô/ do you see?

1. Write the **six** spelling words that have the *au* pattern.

2. Write the **seven** spelling words that have the *o* pattern.

3. Write the **three** spelling words that have the *augh* pattern.

4. Write the **three** spelling words that have the *ough* pattern.

5. Write the **one** spelling word that has the *a* pattern.

Use the steps on page 6 to study words that are hard for you.

Sorting Lists

1. *au* Words
_____
_____
_____
_____
_____
_____

2. *o* Words
_____
_____
_____
_____
_____
_____
_____

3. *augh* Words
_____
_____
_____

4. *ough* Words
_____
_____
_____

5. *a* Word
_____

Spelling Patterns

au	o	augh	ough	a
pause	strong	taught	bought	already

Spelling and Meaning

Classifying Write the spelling word that belongs in each group.

1. instructed, showed, _____
2. clap, cheer, _____
3. powerful, mighty, _____
4. incorrect, mistaken, _____
5. purchased, paid, _____
6. believed, supposed, _____
7. spring, summer, _____
8. captured, grabbed, _____
9. writer, creator, _____
10. stop, rest, _____
11. parent, son, _____
12. delivered, carried, _____
13. give, present, _____

If...Then Write the spelling word that completes each sentence.

14. If Mary jogs four days a week, then she does it _____.
15. If Kara's cat is not here, then it is _____.
16. If Jon is finished with his work, then he's _____ done.
17. If Mom has a special room for working, then she has an _____.
18. If James wins many races, then it's _____ he's a fast runner.
19. If a storm can bend trees, then it might _____ them to fall.

Word Story One spelling word names a bean and the drink made from the bean. Some people think the word comes from the Arabic word *qahwah*, meaning "a strong drink." Write the word.

20. _____

Family Tree: *thought* Think about how the *thought* words are alike in spelling and meaning. Then add another *thought* word to the tree.

rethought

thoughts

thoughtfulness

thoughtful

21.

thought

Use each spelling word once to complete the selection.

Lorraine Hansberry

Lorraine Hansberry was born in Chicago, Illinois, on May 19, 1930. She was

the youngest _____ of Carl and Nannie Hansberry. By the age

1

of 13, Lorraine _____ knew she wanted a job in the theater.

2

After high school Lorraine went to college. There she learned about great

writers and was _____ how to put on plays. Soon she began

3

writing her own plays and moved to New York City. At first she wasn't able to

earn money as an _____. She took odd jobs. She was a clerk in

4

an _____. Then she waited on tables in a _____

5   6

shop, where people _____ breakfast and lunch.

7

In the _____ of 1957, Lorraine read her friends part of a

8

play she'd written. When she finished, they began to _____.

9

Lorraine's friends took the play to some theater people, who agreed to put it

on. The play was called *A Raisin in the Sun*.

Lorraine had very _____ feelings about equal rights. She

10

_____ it was _____ to judge people because of

11   12

their race. The actors in her play talked about those ideas. People were moved

A scene from the movie version of *A Raisin in the Sun*

_____ of the way the feelings of African
<u>13</u>

Americans were explained on the stage.

   A Raisin in the Sun became a hit and _____
                                              <u>14</u>

Lorraine fame and awards. She became the youngest woman and

the first African American woman to receive a major prize for a play.

Soon a film company made her an _____ to make a
                                          <u>15</u>

movie of her play.

   Lorraine then became _____ up in the civil
                              <u>16</u>

rights movement. Because it was a _____ she
                                        <u>17</u>

believed in, she started writing a book about it. But she became ill

and had to _____ in her work.
                <u>18</u>

   In January 1965 Lorraine Hansberry died. Even though she is

_____ , her work still remains. The movie *A Raisin in the*
      <u>19</u>

Sun is _____ shown on TV. A few years ago, Lorraine's
              <u>20</u>

friends produced a play called *To Be Young, Gifted, and Black* about her life.

pause
already
brought
strong
taught
caught
cause
because
wrong
coffee
bought
thought
author
applaud
autumn
daughter
gone
offer
often
office

pause
already
brought
strong
taught
caught
cause
because
wrong
coffee
bought
thought
author
applaud
autumn
daughter
gone
offer
often
office

Write to the Point

Lorraine Hansberry's play *A Raisin in the Sun* was a huge success. Have you seen a play or movie that you'll never forget? Write a review of it that tells what makes it so special. Tell about the acting, costumes, scenery, and whatever else makes the play or movie so outstanding. Try to use spelling words from this lesson.

Use the strategies on page 7 when you are not sure how to spell a word.

Proofreading

Proofread the note below. Use proofreading marks to correct five spelling mistakes, three capitalization mistakes, and two punctuation mistakes.

Proofreading Marks
◯ spell correctly
≡ capitalize
⊙ add period

August 8

Dear mr. Chang,

My mother and I went to the box ofice on main Street and baught tickets for the play Sleeping Beauty. We want to offer you and your daugter two of the tickets She will enjoy the play becawse she offen reads fairy tales with me when she comes over May i bring the tickets to your house tomorrow afternoon?

Keisha

Language Connection

Titles   Underline the titles of books, plays, and movies.

> James and the Giant Peach   The Wizard of Oz

Put quotation marks around the titles of stories, poems, and songs.

> "Hiawatha"   "On Top of Old Smoky"

Capitalize the first, last, and all other important words in a title.

> "Take Me Out to the Ball Game"   The Other Side of the Mountain

Titles are not written correctly in the following sentences, and words are misspelled. Write each sentence correctly.

1. My favorite book, "Harry Potter and the chamber of Secrets," is gonne.

_____

_____

2. Shel Silverstein is the awthor of the poem Recipe for a Hippopotamus Sandwich.

_____

_____

3. Our music teacher tawt us the words to the song city of New Orleans.

_____

_____

Challenge Yourself

Use the Spelling Dictionary to answer these questions. Then use separate paper to write sentences showing that you understand the meaning of each Challenge Word.

Challenge Words

auction	audio
precaution	offerings

4. Does **audio** equipment help people see?   _____

5. Can people buy things at an **auction**?   _____

6. If you give cans of food to help homeless people, are the cans of food your **offerings**?   _____

7. Is locking the door a **precaution** against getting sick?   _____

More Words with /ô/

dawn

Say and Listen

Say each spelling word. Listen for the vowel sound you hear in *lawn*.

Think and Sort

Look at the letters in each word. Think about how the vowel sound in *lawn* is spelled. Spell each word aloud.

The vowel sound in *lawn* can be shown as /ô/. How many spelling patterns for /ô/ do you see?

1. Write the **five** spelling words that have the *aw* pattern.
2. Write the **four** spelling words that have the *a* pattern.
3. Write the **eleven** spelling words that have the *o* pattern.

1. aw Words

_____
_____
_____
_____
_____

2. a Words

_____
_____
_____
_____

3. o Words

_____
_____
_____
_____
_____
_____
_____
_____
_____
_____
_____
_____

lawn
toward
straw
morning
score
north
water
explore
dawn
crawl
quart
warm
before
shore
chorus
yawn
important
orbit
report
popcorn

Use the steps on page 6 to study words that are hard for you.

Spelling Patterns

aw	a	o
lawn	water	north

Spelling and Meaning

Definitions   Write the spelling word for each definition. Use the Spelling Dictionary if you need to.

1. a snack food made from heating corn _____
2. ground that is covered with grass _____
3. dried stalks of grain used for padding _____
4. having great worth or value _____
5. going in the direction of something _____
6. to open the mouth and take in air when tired _____
7. the path of one heavenly body around another _____
8. the number of points made by a player or team _____
9. organized oral or written information _____
10. the first appearance of daylight _____

Analogies   Write the spelling word that completes each analogy.

11. *Evening* is to _____ as *night* is to *day*.
12. *After* is to _____ as *up* is to *down*.
13. *South* is to _____ as *east* is to *west*.
14. *Players* are to *team* as *singers* are to _____.
15. *Find* is to *discover* as *search* is to _____.
16. *Creep* is to _____ as *walk* is to *stroll*.
17. *Dry* is to *wet* as *cool* is to _____.
18. *Pint* is to _____ as *foot* is to *yard*.
19. *Desert* is to *sand* as *lake* is to _____.

Word Story   One spelling word comes from the Old English word *sceran*. *Sceran* meant "to cut." The spelling word means "land at the edge of a sea or lake." Write the word.

20. _____

Family Tree: *explore*   Think about how the *explore* words are alike in spelling and meaning. Then add another *explore* word to the tree.

exploratory

explorer

exploring

21.

explored

explore

Use each spelling word once to complete the story.

Mysteries for the Moonship

One _____ Mr. Goodkind asked his students to go on
                    1

a scavenger hunt. He divided the class into teams. Each team decided on a

name for themselves. Zachary, Katy, Mark, and Amanda chose Moonship as

their team name. Then Mr. Goodkind gave each team a list of things to find.

The Moonship team began to groan. Their list was hidden in three riddles.

Mark read the first riddle:

> Let the pan go from _____ to hot,
>   2
> And into _____ I am shot.
>   3
> Sputter, sputter, pour on the butter!

"Let's go!" Zachary said. "Maybe the answer will pop into our heads. Pop . . .

_____!"
        4

"Popcorn's the answer!" the team shouted.

Moonship headed _____ Mark's house to get some popcorn.
                              5

They found a _____ of milk and drank it. Then Mark's dad helped
                    6

them pop some popcorn. They washed the milk carton with _____
                                                              7

and put the popcorn in. The second riddle was harder:

> From _____ to dark I nibble and _____.
>   8   9
> My soft fuzzy body is low and small.
>
> When the time comes, I spin a soft wrap.
>
> I _____ and curl up inside for a nap.
>   10
> I wake up and am not what I was before.
>
> I've beautiful wings and the sky to _____.
>   11

"A baby takes a nap and crawls," said Mark. "Hey, Zachary!

Stop eating our popcorn. This is _____. Think!"
                                              12

"I am thinking about how good this popcorn would taste if

it had some butter on it. Butter . . . butterfly!" Zachary exclaimed.

"No. But caterpillar is the answer!" said Amanda.

The Moonship team searched until they found a caterpillar near

the _____ of the pond at the city park. From there
          13

they headed _____ to Katy's house.
                    14

Katy read the next riddle:

In spring I rise, damp and green.

In a place like a _____ is where I am seen.
                          15

Yet soon I'm a basket, I'm a hat.

I'm a broom, I'm a welcome mat.

Scarecrows and haystacks are made from me.

Burning matches I hate to see.

"_____!" the Moonship team sang out in
        16

_____ as they grabbed a broom from the kitchen.
        17

With the straw broom, caterpillar, and popcorn, they raced

back to school. Soon they arrived at their classroom

to _____ to Mr. Goodkind.
        18

"Well, Moonship," Mr. Goodkind said.

"You got here _____ the
                      19

others. Your team will get a perfect

_____! It looks like the
        20

Moonship made the first landing!"

lawn
toward
straw
morning
score
north
water
explore
dawn
crawl
quart
warm
before
shore
chorus
yawn
important
orbit
report
popcorn

lawn
toward
straw
morning
score
north
water
explore
dawn
crawl
quart
warm
before
shore
chorus
yawn
important
orbit
report
popcorn

Write to the Point

Mr. Goodkind made his students think by giving them riddles that described different things. Write two riddles like the ones Mr. Goodkind wrote for the scavenger hunt. Then see if your classmates can guess what you describe in your riddles. Try to use spelling words from this lesson.

Use the strategies on page 7 when you are not sure how to spell a word.

Proofreading

Proofread the newspaper article below. Use proofreading marks to correct five spelling mistakes, three capitalization mistakes, and two missing words.

Proofreading Marks
◯ spell correctly
≡ capitalize
∧ add

The McHenry School Report

Class Trip Big Success

One morning last week, mr. Goodkind took his students to shore along Long Beach. The bus left at doun and headed narth. The students rushed off the bus with a choras of cheers. then they ran tord the water to explore a long stretch of sandy beach.

Two students had never been to the beach befour. everyone had great time.

Language Connection

Commas   Use a comma between the city and the state and between the day and the year.

| Tipton, Indiana | | February 29, 2004 |

In a friendly letter, use a comma after the last word of the greeting and closing.

| Dear Elliot, | | Your friend, |

Add commas where they are needed in the letter below. Also find the misspelled words and write them correctly on the lines provided.

2036 Circle Loop Drive

Richmond VA 23294

June 23 2003

Dear Donna

    We're here at the lake, and it's really great. Our cabin is right on the shure. We have a view of the watter from every room.

    I plan to eksplore the woods around us tomorrow morening. It has been really waurm here. The weather repourt says the rest of the week will be sunny and hot. What perfect weather for a summer vacation!

Yours truly

Dawn

1. _____   2. _____   3. _____

4. _____   5. _____   6. _____

Challenge Yourself

What do you think each Challenge Word means? Check the Spelling Dictionary to see if you are right. Then use separate paper to write sentences showing that you understand the meaning of each Challenge Word.

Challenge Words

| adorn | awesome |
| hoard | torture |

7. Jasper spends his allowance, but Kendra likes to **hoard** hers.

8. The view from the mountain was an **awesome** sight.

9. We decided to **adorn** the class float with ribbons and flowers.

10. It was **torture** to hike five miles in the hot sun.

Words with /är/ or /âr/

marbles

1. /är/ Words

_____
_____
_____
_____
_____
_____
_____

2. /âr/ Words

_____
_____
_____
_____
_____
_____
_____
_____
_____
_____
_____
_____

sharp

share

they're

marbles

their

where

smart

large

heart

careful

square

there

stairs

fair

air

fare

stares

scarf

apart

alarm

Say and Listen

The spelling words for this lesson contain the /är/ and /âr/ sounds that you hear in *sharp* and *share.* Say the spelling words. Listen for the /är/ and /âr/ sounds.

Think and Sort

Look at the letters in each word. Think about how the /är/ or /âr/ sounds are spelled. Spell each word aloud. How many spelling patterns for /är/ and /âr/ do you see?

1. The /är/ sounds can be spelled *ar* or *ear.* Write the **eight** /är/ spelling words. Circle the letters that spell /är/ in each word.

2. The /âr/ sounds can be spelled *are, air, ere, eir,* or *ey're.* Write the **twelve** /âr/ spelling words. Circle the letters that spell /âr/ in each word.

Use the steps on page 6 to study words that are hard for you.

Spelling Patterns

/är/	ar	ear			
	sharp	heart			
/âr/	are	air	ere	eir	ey're
	share	fair	there	their	they're

Spelling and Meaning

Classifying   Write the spelling word that belongs in each group.

1. wind, breeze, _____
2. thorny, pointed, _____
3. bell, siren, _____
4. hat, gloves, _____
5. bright, clever, _____
6. big, huge, _____
7. separated, in pieces, _____
8. slow, watchful, _____
9. triangle, rectangle, _____
10. give, divide, _____
11. jacks, checkers, _____
12. who, what, _____

Homophones   Complete each sentence with the spelling word that is a homophone of the underlined word.

13. Steven and Jake left _____ shoes over <u>there</u>.
14. The high <u>fare</u> for the plane trip is not _____.
15. Elena <u>stares</u> at the seven flights of _____.
16. The bus _____ to the <u>fair</u> was cheap.
17. <u>They're</u> waiting over _____ by the bench.
18. Today _____ bringing <u>their</u> projects to school.
19. Jess _____ at the ball as it bounces down the <u>stairs</u>.

Word Story   The phrase "raining cats and dogs" is an **idiom**. The meanings of the words in an idiom don't add up to the meaning of the idiom. Write the spelling word that completes the following idiom.

   I know that song by _____.

20. _____

Family Tree: *fair*   Think about how the *fair* words are alike in spelling and meaning. Then add another *fair* word to the tree.

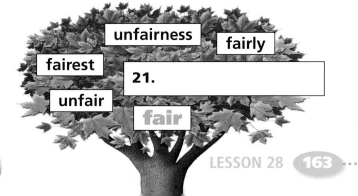

unfairness   fairly
fairest
21.
unfair
fair

Use each spelling word once to complete the story.

The Marble Contest

Charlie woke at once when his _____
1
went off. It was the morning of the marble contest. He reached under his bed for his _____ and carefully placed
2
his lucky one in a box. Then he wrapped a big handful of them in an old red _____, dressed quickly, and ran down the back
3
_____ to grab some breakfast.
4

"Got everything you need?" his mother asked.

"You bet, Ma. I've got all of them ready to go. My lucky one is packed in a box. Can't take a chance on losing that one!"

"Oh, Charlie! You're a _____ boy. You know that skill
5
wins a game, not luck," his mother said.

Charlie ate his toast and eggs and gathered his belongings. He was _____ not to drop the small _____ box that
6   7
held his lucky marble.

The crisp autumn _____ hummed with excitement, and
8
Charlie's _____ pounded as he got closer to the center of
9
town. A very _____ group of boys had gathered in the
10
village square. _____ faces grew serious as Charlie came
11
near. He met their _____. After all, he was the champion!
12

"Look at that crowd over _____," his friend Jess shouted.
13

"_____ waiting for us."
14

The boys gathered around a circle in the dirt and soon were shooting marbles with quick, _____ 15 flicks of their fingers. When the marbles were knocked _____ 16 , laughs and shouts went through the group.

As the day wore on, players were eliminated. Charlie and Jess were alone around the circle. Those who lost stayed to _____ 17 the thrill of the last match. Charlie pulled out the box to place his lucky marble beside him.

" _____ 18 is my tiger's-eye marble? Hold on! This isn't _____ 19 ! I must have left it at home!" he said. But Jess and all of the boys wanted the game to go on.

"How could I have done this?" Charlie wondered. "OK, Ma. Now let's see what skill can do!" He aimed a marble at the center and closed his eyes. The marbles clicked, and a cheer rose from the crowd.

"The winner and still champion, Charlie Coleman!"

Charlie's prize was his _____ 20 to the statewide marble contest in St. Louis. Charlie grinned and looked at Jess. "I'll take my tiger's-eye marble to St. Louis," he said. "But who needs a lucky marble when you've got skill?"

sharp
share
they're
marbles
their
where
smart
large
heart
careful
square
there
stairs
fair
air
fare
stares
scarf
apart
alarm

sharp
share
they're
marbles
their
where
smart
large
heart
careful
square
there
stairs
fair
air
fare
stares
scarf
apart
alarm

Write to the Point

Sometimes the simplest games, like marbles, jacks, and tag, are the most fun to play. Think of a game you know that is simple enough to explain in a few sentences. Then write a paragraph telling how to play it. Make your instructions easy to follow. Try to use spelling words from this lesson.

Use the strategies on page 7 when you are not sure how to spell a word.

Proofreading

Proofread the directions below. Use proofreading marks to correct five spelling mistakes, three capitalization mistakes, and two unnecessary words.

Proofreading Marks
◯ spell correctly
≡ capitalize
؋ take out

How to Play Hide-and-Seek

Here's how you play hide-and-seek. first, cover your your eyes with a skarf. Then tell everybody to hide while you count to fifty. Be carful not to peek. are you smeart enough to find them? Don't forget to look under under the stairs. Remember to push larje bushes apheart. Look until you find someone. then that person's It and has to find someone.

Dictionary Skills

Pronunciation   A dictionary lists a pronunciation, or sound spelling, for most entry words. Special symbols are used to show the pronunciation. These symbols are listed in the pronunciation key.

stare (stâr) *v.* **stared, star·ing, stares.**
To look at with a steady gaze: *Jasmine stared at the famous movie star. These sound alike:* **stare, stair.**

Pronunciation Key

ă	pat	ŏ	pot	ŭ	cut
ā	pay	ō	toe	ûr	urge
âr	care	ô	paw, for	ə	about,
ä	father	oi	noise		item,
ĕ	pet	ŏŏ	took		edible,
ē	bee	ōō	boot		gallop,
ĭ	pit	ou	out		circus
ī	pie	th	thin	ər	butter
îr	deer	*th*	**this**		

Write the correct word for each pronunciation. Use the Spelling Dictionary and the pronunciation key.

1. (wâr) _____
2. (härt) _____
3. (ə **lärm′**) _____
4. (âr) _____
5. (shärp) _____
6. (shâr) _____
7. (skärf) _____
8. (smärt) _____
9. (ə **pärt′**) _____
10. (**mär′** bəls) _____
11. (skwâr) _____
12. (**kâr′** fəl) _____

Challenge Yourself

What do you think each Challenge Word means? Check the Spelling Dictionary to see if you are right. Then use separate paper to write sentences showing that you understand the meaning of each Challenge Word.

Challenge Words
collage   airborne
regardless   varnish

13. We used string, colored paper, and buttons to make a **collage** to hang on the wall.

14. I could not see the **airborne** dust, but it made me sneeze.

15. The picnic will be held today, **regardless** of the weather.

16. The coat of **varnish** made the desk shine as if it were new.

Lesson 29

Plural and Possessive Words

sheep

1. Plural Nouns

_____
_____
_____
_____
_____
_____
_____
_____
_____
_____
_____
_____

2. Possessive Nouns

_____
_____
_____
_____
_____
_____
_____
_____

children
men
shelves
man's
cloud's
women
feet
woman's
women's
child's
teeth
children's
sheep
oxen
mice
geese
wife's
knives
wives
men's

Say and Listen

Say each spelling word. Listen to the sounds in each word.

Think and Sort

Some of the spelling words are **plural nouns.** They name more than one person, place, or thing. The usual way to form the plural of a noun is to add -s or -es. The plural nouns in this lesson are not formed in that way. They are called **irregular plurals.**

The other spelling words show ownership. They are called **possessive nouns.** How do all of these words end?

Look at each spelling word. Spell each word aloud.

1. Write the **twelve** spelling words that are plural nouns.

2. Write the **eight** spelling words that are possessive nouns.

Use the steps on page 6 to study words that are hard for you.

Spelling Patterns

Plurals		
men	children	wives
Possessives		
man's	child's	wife's
men's	children's	

Spelling and Meaning

Analogies   Write the spelling word that completes each analogy.

1. *Horses* are to *hay* as _____ are to *cheese.*

2. *Drawers* are to *dressers* as _____ are to *bookcases.*

3. *Alligators* are to *reptiles* as _____ are to *birds.*

4. *Kittens* are to *cats* as *lambs* are to _____.

5. *Lawnmowers* are to *grass* as _____ are to *food.*

6. *Fingers* are to *hands* as *toes* are to _____.

7. *Floors* are to *mop* as _____ are to *brush.*

8. *Mothers* are to *women* as *fathers* are to _____.

9. *Child* is to *children* as *ox* is to _____.

10. *Gentlemen* are to *men* as *ladies* are to _____.

11. *Ducklings* are to *ducks* as _____ are to *humans.*

Trading Places   Write the possessive word that can be used instead of the underlined words.

12. the shoes <u>belonging to the man</u>   the _____ shoes

13. the toy <u>belonging to the child</u>   the _____ toy

14. the parents <u>of the wife</u>   the _____ parents

15. the shape <u>of the cloud</u>   the _____ shape

16. the dresses <u>belonging to the women</u>   the _____ dresses

17. the books <u>belonging to the children</u>   the _____ books

18. the hands <u>of the men</u>   the _____ hands

19. the face <u>of the woman</u>   the _____ face

Word Story   One spelling word comes from the Old English word *wif.* Long ago *wif* simply meant "a woman." Today the spelling word means " married women." Write the word.

20. _____

Family Tree: *children*   *Children* is a form of *child.* Think about how the *child* words are alike in spelling and meaning. Then add another *child* word to the tree.

childless

children

childishly

21.

childlike

child

Use each spelling word once to complete the story.

In Someone Else's Shoes

There once lived a man named Manuel who had a wife, Alma, and four _____ . Every day Manuel went

1

into the fields to work, like the other _____ . Alma stayed at home,

2

like the other _____ . One day Manuel said that his work was

3

hard, while his _____ work was easy.

4

Alma looked at Manuel and said, "I wonder what would happen if husbands

and _____ traded places."

5

Manuel laughed and then said to Alma, "Let's trade work, and you will see

how hard a _____ life really is."

6

His wife answered, "You may discover that a _____ life

7

is not so easy, either." Alma hitched up the _____ and set

8

off for the fields.

In the meantime, Manuel began to make the _____ breakfast

9

and told them to brush their _____ . It seemed to Manuel that as

10

soon as he had taken care of one _____ needs, another wanted

11

his help. He left the house and began the chores.

First he scattered grain for the _____ . Then he fed the cows.

12

Manuel didn't feed the cats, since they were busy chasing _____ .

13

Just as he began to put the _____ out to pasture, he heard the

14

children yelling. Manuel didn't know how he could watch both the children and the

sheep, so he carried the sheep up to the grass roof to graze. He tied ropes around

their legs and dropped the ropes down the chimney. He rushed to the kitchen and

tied a rope around each of his legs so that the sheep could not run away. Then Manuel went back to work. He washed the dishes, forks, and _____. He had begun to put them on the kitchen
15

_____ when the sheep fell off the roof. Manuel
16

went _____-first up the chimney!
17

Out in the fields, Alma stopped working. She looked up at the sky and noticed a large _____ dark color.
18
Alma knew that it was going to rain. Many of the men were already heading home. Judging that her wagon was as full as the _____
19
wagons, she went home, too.

When she opened the door, Alma saw Manuel hanging upside down in the fireplace and the children running wildly about. Quickly she grabbed a knife and cut the rope.

"Well," she asked, "how do you like _____
20
work?"

Manuel never said a word about women's work again.

children
men
shelves
man's
cloud's
women
feet
woman's
women's
child's
teeth
children's
sheep
oxen
mice
geese
wife's
knives
wives
men's

children
men
shelves
man's
cloud's
women
feet
woman's
women's
child's
teeth
children's
sheep
oxen
mice
geese
wife's
knives
wives
men's

Write to the Point

Manuel and Alma traded places. Is there someone with whom you would like to trade places? Write a paragraph telling with whom you would like to trade places and why. Try to use spelling words from this lesson.

Use the strategies on page 7 when you are not sure how to spell a word.

Proofreading

Proofread the list below. Use proofreading marks to correct five spelling mistakes, three capitalization mistakes, and two unnecessary words.

Proofreading Marks
◯ spell correctly
≡ capitalize
ℒ take out

Things to Do

1. Polish mother's knifs, forks, and spoons.

2. Help jacob build a pen for the gooses.

3. Find a mans' suit for for the school play.

4. Wash the kitchen shelfes.

5. Write a report on sheeps for Mr. rice's class.

6. See dr. Keith to to have my teeth cleaned.

Language Connection

Possessive Nouns   An apostrophe is used to show possession, or ownership.
Add 's to a singular noun to make it possessive.

> the boy**'s** hat = the hat that belongs to the boy
>
> the child**'s** toy = the toy that belongs to the child

Add only an apostrophe to a plural noun that ends in s.
Add 's to a plural noun that does not end in s.

> The boys**'** sleds are red.   The children**'s** sleds are fast.

Complete each sentence with the correct word from the boxes.

 woman's   women   women's

1. This _____ car has broken down on the highway.

2. Those two _____ jog every morning along the lake.

3. These _____ gardens are large and beautiful.

 child's   children   children's

4. The _____ all play together every day in the park.

5. Three _____ lunches were missing from the shelf.

6. One _____ jacket sleeve is ripped.

Challenge Yourself

Write the Challenge Word for each clue. Check the Spelling
Dictionary to see if you are right. Then use separate paper to
write sentences showing that you understand the meaning
of each Challenge Word.

Challenge Words	
larvae	thieves
mongoose's	patios

7. They take things that don't belong to them.   _____

8. These are places outside where you can relax.   _____

9. This means "belonging to a kind of mammal that kills snakes."

_____

10. These will soon change into something very different.   _____

Lesson 30

Unit 5 Review
Lessons 25–29

Use the steps on page 6 to study words that are hard for you

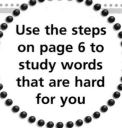

25

loyal
choice

Words with /oi/

Complete each sentence by writing the spelling word that rhymes with the underlined word.

1. If you lose your <u>voice</u>, you have no _____ but to whisper.

2. The prince's _____ dog guarded the <u>royal</u> palace.

26

autumn
daughter
wrong
often
bought
already

Words with /ô/

Write the spelling word for each clue.

3. Leaves fall off trees in this season. _____

4. If you are not right, you are this. _____

5. A parent's female child is this. _____

6. This means the same as purchased. _____

7. This means you've done something many times. _____

8. This means something has happened in the past.

_____

27

dawn
toward
explore
important

More Words with /ô/

Write the spelling word that completes each sentence.

9. The ocean is most beautiful at _____.

10. Kevin walked slowly _____ the frightened puppy.

11. You have an _____ decision to make.

12. Let's _____ those caves today.

28 marbles
heart
careful
square
stairs
where
their
they're

Words with /är/ or /âr/

Write the spelling word that completes each analogy.

13. *Dinner* is to *supper* as _____ are to *steps*.

14. *Hair* is to *hare* as *wear* is to _____.

15. *Mean* is to *cruel* as _____ is to *watchful*.

16. *Sphere* is to *circle* as *cube* is to _____.

17. *Brain* is to *think* as _____ is to *pump*.

18. *We have* is to *we've* as *they are* is to _____.

19. *Baseball* is to *sport* as _____ are to *game*.

20. *We* is to *our* as *they* is to _____.

29 geese
oxen
wives
wife's
men's

Plural and Possessive Words

Write the spelling word that belongs in each group.

21. ducks, swans, _____

22. husbands, children, _____

23. husband's, child's, _____

24. women's, children's, _____

25. mules, cows, _____

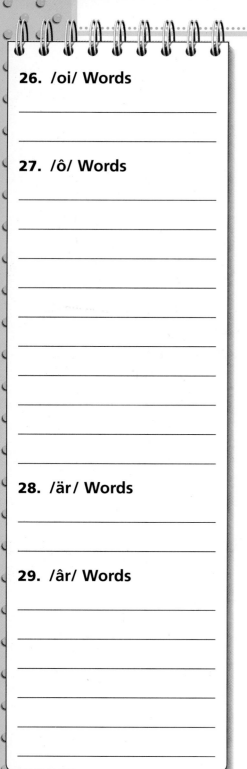

26. /oi/ Words

_____

_____

27. /ô/ Words

_____

_____

_____

_____

_____

_____

_____

_____

_____

_____

28. /är/ Words

_____

_____

29. /âr/ Words

_____

_____

_____

_____

_____

_____

Review Sort

autumn	already	they're	heart
wrong	their	marbles	loyal
careful	bought	toward	choice
often	daughter	dawn	explore
important	stairs	square	where

26. Write the **two** /oi/ words. Circle the letters that spell /oi/ in each word.

27. Write the **ten** /ô/ words. Circle the letter or letters that spell /ô/ in each word.

28. Write the **two** /är/ words. Circle the letters that spell /är/ in each word.

29. Write the **six** /âr/ words. Circle the letters that spell /âr/ in each word.

These four words have been sorted into two groups. Explain how the words in each group are alike.

30. woman's   man's

_____

_____

31. women's   men's

_____

_____

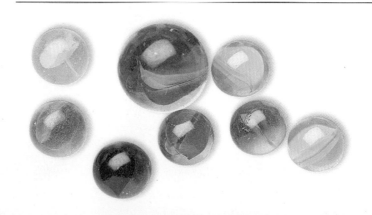

Writer's Workshop

Instructions

Instructions tell a reader how to do something. Good instructions carefully describe each step. They include all important details. Words like *first*, *then*, and *next* can help the reader move from step to step. Here are Arturo's instructions on how to stand on your head.

Prewriting To write his instructions, Arturo followed the steps in the writing process. After he decided on a topic, he completed a how-to chart. On the chart he listed each step. The chart helped Arturo make sure his instructions were clear and complete. Part of Arturo's how-to chart is shown here. Study what Arturo did.

How to Stand on Your Head

Standing on your head is easy once you get the feel of it. First, get on your knees and put the top of your head on a pillow. Then put your palms flat on the floor, slightly in front of your head. Next, raise your knees and rest them on your elbows. Slowly straighten your back and bring your knees together. Finally, straighten your legs. You're upside down!

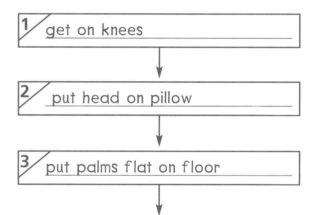

1. get on knees
2. put head on pillow
3. put palms flat on floor

It's Your Turn!

Write your own instructions. You can tell how to make something, how to play a game, or anything you wish. Once you have decided on a topic, make a how-to chart. Start at the beginning and be sure to include every important step. Then follow the other steps in the writing process—writing, revising, proofreading, and publishing. Try to use spelling words from this lesson in your instructions.

Lesson 31

Words with /ûr/ or /îr/

circus

1. /ûr/ Words

_____
_____
_____
_____
_____
_____
_____
_____
_____
_____
_____
_____
_____
_____

2. /îr/ Words

_____
_____
_____
_____
_____
_____

curve
hear
clear
learn
third
dear
circus
skirt
heard
squirt
early
birth
germ
world
cheer
period
here
circle
earn
dirty

Say and Listen

The spelling words for this lesson contain the /ûr/ or /îr/ sounds that you hear in *curve* and *hear.* Say the spelling words. Listen for the /ûr/ and /îr/ sounds.

Think and Sort

Look at the letters in each word. Think about how the /ûr/ or /îr/ sounds are spelled. Spell each word aloud.

How many spelling patterns for /ûr/ and /îr/ do you see?

1. Write the **fourteen** spelling words that have the /ûr/ sounds. Circle the letters that spell /ûr/ in each word.

2. Write the **six** spelling words that have the /îr/ sounds. Circle the letters that spell /îr/ in each word.

Use the steps on page 6 to study words that are hard for you.

Spelling Patterns

/ûr/	/îr/
curve skirt learn	hear period
world germ	here cheer

Spelling and Meaning

Synonyms   Write the spelling word that is a synonym for each word.

1. bend _____
2. plain _____
3. yell _____
4. soiled _____

Analogies   Write the spelling word that completes each analogy.

5. *Continent* is to _____ as *county* is to *state*.
6. *Ending* is to *death* as *beginning* is to _____.
7. *Too* is to *two* as *deer* is to _____.
8. *Now* is to *then* as _____ is to *there*.
9. *Listened* is to _____ as *story* is to *tale*.
10. *Spend* is to _____ as *give* is to *get*.
11. *Speak* is to *mouth* as _____ is to *ear*.
12. *Door* is to *rectangle* as *plate* is to _____.
13. *Ask* is to *question mark* as *tell* is to _____.
14. *Two* is to *second* as *three* is to _____.
15. *Pour* is to *milk* as _____ is to *toothpaste*.
16. *Blouse* is to *top* as _____ is to *bottom*.
17. *School* is to _____ as *office* is to *work*.
18. *Sad* is to *happy* as *late* is to _____.
19. *Microscope* is to _____ as *telescope* is to *star*.

Word Story   One spelling word comes from the Greek word for *circle, kirkos*. The spelling word names a kind of entertainment that is presented inside circular rings. Write the word.

20. _____

Family Tree: *cheer*   Think about how the *cheer* words are alike in spelling and meaning. Then add another *cheer* word to the tree.

cheerfully

cheerful

cheering

21.

cheers

cheery

cheer

Spelling in Context

Use each spelling word once to complete the selection.

The Circus, Past and Present

People clap and _____. Elephants parade and bow.
1

Clowns _____ water in each other's face. A woman in a
2

shiny satin _____ rides on a galloping white horse. You can
3

_____ lively music played on an organ and steam whistles.
4

Where are you? You are at the _____!
5

The circus as we know it began in England more than 200 years ago. A man

named Philip Astley started performing riding tricks. He stood on his horse's back

as the horse trotted in a _____. This was the
6

first circus ring. Astley's act was exciting, but one thing soon

became _____ to him. He needed more acts.
7

He added acrobats, a clown, and a band. The crowd loved the show, and

the circus was born!

The _____ of the circus was also the beginning of
8

many circus traditions. One tradition is that the acts are performed in a

ring. Most _____ circuses had only one or two rings.
9

After a _____ of time, circuses grew larger. They added
10

a _____ ring—and more acts.
11

At the first circuses, clowns kept people laughing. Early clowns wore dressy clothes. Some later clowns dressed in wild outfits with bright colors. Others dressed in _____ 12 rags to look like "tramps."

Being in a circus is a way of life. Modern circus people travel _____ 13 and there all over the countryside. They work together like members of a large family. The adults help children _____ 14 to juggle, to ride, and to care for the animals. Animals that are poorly fed do not perform well. Neither do animals that get sick from a harmful _____ 15 in a dirty stall.

Many circus children grow up and _____ 16 their living by doing the same act their parents did. You may have _____ 17 of circus families who have performed the same act for years and years. Horses and trick riders are as important in today's circus as they were in Astley's show. It takes skill to stay on a galloping horse when it turns a sharp _____ 18 !

Adults and children now enjoy the circus in countries all around the _____ 19 . Going to the circus is a childhood memory many adults hold _____ 20 . They want their children to enjoy the same happy experience.

curve
hear
clear
learn
third
dear
circus
skirt
heard
squirt
early
birth
germ
world
cheer
period
here
circle
earn
dirty

Spelling and Writing

curve
hear
clear
learn
third
dear
circus
skirt
heard
squirt
early
birth
germ
world
cheer
period
here
circle
earn
dirty

Write to the Point

Write a paragraph about a job that you would like to have at a circus. Give reasons why you would like the job and why you would be good at it. Try to use spelling words from this lesson.

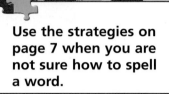

Use the strategies on page 7 when you are not sure how to spell a word.

Proofreading

Proofread the e-mail below. Use proofreading marks to correct five spelling mistakes, three capitalization mistakes, and two unnecessary words.

Proofreading Marks
◯ spell correctly
≡ capitalize
℘ take out

e-mail
Address Book Attachment Check Spelling Send Save Draft Cancel

Hi, Wanda!

For my birthday Dad took me to the circas. we saw

a funny clown with durty white shoes. His name was

dr. Sneezo. He chased a a giant germ in a circel and

tried to squert it with a bottle of green medicine. the crowd

would would chear every time Dr. Sneezo tried to hit the

germ. He never did it. That germ was just too fast for

him. Dad and I had a great time.

Tina

Language Connection

Plurals   Plurals are words that name more than one thing. Most plurals are formed by adding -s or -es to the base word.

> To form the plural of most nouns, add -s.
>
> cheer + s = cheer**s**   circle + s = circle**s**
>
> If the noun ends in s, x, ch, sh, or z, add -es.
>
> fox + **es** = fox**es**   bus + **es** = bus**es**

Write the plural form of each word.

1. curve _____

2. birth _____

3. circus _____

4. brush _____

5. skirt _____

6. match _____

7. germ _____

8. box _____

9. world _____

10. animal _____

11. period _____

12. horse _____

13. circle _____

14. ax _____

15. branch _____

16. dress _____

17. cheer _____

18. glass _____

19. inch _____

20. buzz _____

Challenge Yourself

Use the Spelling Dictionary to answer these questions. Then use separate paper to write sentences showing that you understand the meaning of each Challenge Word.

> **Challenge Words**
>
> courtesy   convert
> worthwhile   interior

21. Should you go outside to see the **interior** of a building? _____

22. When you thank someone for a gift, are you showing **courtesy**? _____

23. Can you **convert** a piece of rock into gold? _____

24. If you went to a store but found that it was closed, was the trip **worthwhile**? _____

automobile

1. Words with One /ə/

_____
_____
_____
_____
_____
_____
_____
_____
_____
_____
_____
_____
_____
_____

2. Words with More than One /ə/

_____
_____
_____
_____
_____
_____

together
animal
blizzard
simple
wrinkle
United States
   of America
calendar
special
winter
summer
automobile
dinosaur
Canada
address
chapter
whether
whistle
purple
tickle
wander

Say and Listen

Say the spelling words. Listen for the syllables that are not stressed.

Think and Sort

Most unstressed syllables have a weak vowel sound called **schwa**. It is shown as /ə/. Some words have one /ə/, and others have more than one.

Look at the letters in each word as you say each word again. Think about how /ə/ is spelled. Spell each word aloud. How many spelling patterns for /ə/ do you see?

1. Write the **fourteen** spelling words that have one /ə/ sound. Circle the letter that spells /ə/.

2. Write the **six** spelling words that have more than one /ə/ sound. Circle the letters that spell /ə/.

> Use the steps on page 6 to study words that are hard for you.

Spelling Patterns

a	e	i	o
address	summer	animal	dinosaur

Spelling and Meaning

Classifying   Write the spelling word that belongs in each group.

1. red, blue, _____

2. hurricane, tornado, _____

3. easy, plain, _____

4. crease, crumple, _____

5. name, _____, telephone number

6. roam, stray, _____

7. train, plane, _____

8. beast, creature, _____

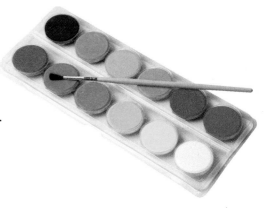

Definitions   Write the spelling word for each definition.
Use the Spelling Dictionary if you need to.

9. at the same time _____

10. if _____

11. North American country containing fifty states _____

12. a main division of a book _____

13. the season between fall and spring _____

14. northernmost North American country _____

15. chart showing time by days, weeks, and months _____

16. not usual _____

17. the season between spring and fall _____

18. to touch lightly _____

19. to make a sound by forcing air through lips _____

Word Story   One spelling word comes from two Greek words, *deinos* and *saurus*. *Deinos* meant "terrible" and *saurus* meant "lizard." Write the word.

20. _____

Family Tree: *simple*   Think about how the *simple* words are alike in spelling and meaning. Then add another *simple* word to the tree.

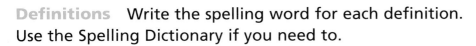

simpler

simplify

simplified

21.

simply

simple

You Won't See This at the Zoo!

Can you picture an elephant covered with fur? Does it _____ you to think of a horse the size of a dog or a rhino taller than a two-story building? These creatures do not come from a _____ of a science fiction book. They are real! They lived in an age that is not part of any _____. This age was long before recorded time.

Suppose that you could go back 55 million years in time. The climate is like _____ all year round. The world's first horses are grazing in the grass among pink and _____ flowers. You might wonder _____ or not they really are horses. They are only a foot tall. They look like tiny deer.

Thirty million years later, you can see the largest land mammal of all time. It is a giant, hornless rhinoceros.

It stands about eighteen feet tall and has loose skin that folds

like a giant _____ at each joint. You could easily
                    7

drive an _____ right under this huge creature!
                8

    If you travel forward in time to the Ice Age, you will find

a snowy world. Here it is _____ all the time.
                                  9

Icy winds _____ through the trees. Only the
                10

huge furry mammoths brave the _____. They
                                        11

move _____ in a herd and search for food.
            12

The mammoths have _____ bodies that are
                          13

made for the cold. They are covered with warm, shaggy

fur. The mammoths live throughout North America. Their

fossils will be found in both _____ and the
                                    14

_____.
        15

    Two million years later, you can watch an enormous

armadillo _____ slowly through the grasslands
                16

of South America. This _____ has leathery skin
                            17

and bony spikes on its tail. It looks like a stegosaurus, but it is

not a _____ at all.
            18

    All of the prehistoric animals have disappeared from the

earth. You can still learn about them, though. It

is a _____ thing to do. Look
            19

for the place where they still come

alive. Just find the _____
                            20

of a library near you!

together
animal
blizzard
simple
wrinkle
United States
    of America
calendar
special
winter
summer
automobile
dinosaur
Canada
address
chapter
whether
whistle
purple
tickle
wander

Spelling and Writing

together
animal
blizzard
simple
wrinkle
United States
    of America
calendar
special
winter
summer
automobile
dinosaur
Canada
address
chapter
whether
whistle
purple
tickle
wander

Write to the Point

In "You Won't See This at the Zoo!" you read about animals that lived before recorded time. Choose a prehistoric animal and write a short description that tells what it looked like. Try to use spelling words from this lesson.

Use the strategies on page 7 when you are not sure how to spell a word.

Proofreading

Proofread the list below. Use proofreading marks to correct five spelling mistakes, three capitalization mistakes, and two unnecessary words.

Proofreading Marks
◯ spell correctly
≡ capitalize
ℰ take out

Things to Do for My Art Projects

1. paint a picture of a dinosar.

2. Make lots of grass and and trees around it for its

   sumer home.

3. tape boxes tagether to make the body of a mammoth.

4. Cover the mammoth's body with strips of newspaper

   dipped in in paste.

5. glue on yarn to make its speshal covering.

6. Use white cotton balls to make the

   mammoth's wintur home.

Dictionary Skills

Accent Marks   Special symbols are often used in dictionaries to show the pronunciation of words. The schwa (ə) is a symbol for the weak vowel sound that occurs in unstressed syllables. The accent mark (') is used to point out syllables that are spoken with more stress, or force. Some dictionaries also use dark type to show accented syllables.

Only one of the pronunciations in each pair below has the accent mark on the correct syllable. Circle the correct pronunciation and write the word. Check your answers in the Spelling Dictionary.

1. /**blĭz′** ərd/   /**blĭz** ərd′/   _____
2. /**ăn′** ə məl/   /**ăn** ə **məl′**/   _____
3. /wĭs əl′/   /**wĭs′** əl/   _____
4. /tĭk əl′/   /**tĭk′** əl/   _____
5. /**sĭm′** pəl/   /**sĭm** pəl′/   _____
6. /**rĭng′** kəl/   /**rĭng** kəl′/   _____
7. /kăl ən′ dər/   /**kăl′** ən dər/   _____
8. /**sŭm′** ər/   /**sŭm** ər′/   _____
9. /pûr **pəl′**/   /**pûr′** pəl/   _____

Challenge Yourself

Write the Challenge Word for each clue. Check the Spelling Dictionary to see if you are right. Then use separate paper to write sentences showing that you understand the meaning of each Challenge Word.

Challenge Words	
burglar	missile
binoculars	dwindle

10. Things look closer when you look through these.

    _____

11. This can be fired at a target that is far away.   _____

12. This is someone who breaks into a house to steal something.

    _____

13. The library's supply of books will do this if everyone checks out books.

    _____

Compound Words

basketball

1. _____
2. _____
3. _____
4. _____
5. _____
6. _____
7. _____
8. _____
9. _____
10. _____
11. _____
12. _____
13. _____
14. _____
15. _____
16. _____
17. _____
18. _____
19. _____
20. _____

basketball
cheeseburger
countdown
newspaper
drugstore
outside
everybody
birthday
upstairs
inside
nightmare
afternoon
anything
forever
sometimes
weekend
downtown
without
everywhere
railroad

Say and Listen

Say each spelling word. Listen for the two shorter words in each word.

Think and Sort

All of the spelling words are compound words. In a **compound word**, two words are joined to form a new word. For example, *basket + ball = basketball.* Write the spelling word that is formed from each word pair below.

1. after + noon
2. any + thing
3. for + ever
4. some + times
5. with + out
6. every + body
7. basket + ball
8. count + down
9. in + side
10. out + side
11. night + mare
12. news + paper
13. up + stairs
14. drug + store
15. every + where
16. rail + road
17. week + end
18. birth + day
19. down + town
20. cheese + burger

Use the steps on page 6 to study words that are hard for you.

Spelling Patterns

| basket\|ball | every\|body | down\|town | for\|ever |

Spelling and Meaning

Antonyms Complete each sentence by writing the spelling word that is an antonym of the underlined word.

1. The museum is <u>uptown</u>, but the library is _____.
2. John likes eggs <u>with</u> salt but _____ pepper.
3. I went <u>downstairs</u> as Maria went _____.
4. Customers are _____, but a clerk is <u>nowhere</u> to be found.
5. We couldn't play <u>outside</u>, so we went _____.

Compound Words Write the spelling word that can be formed by combining two words in each sentence.

6. Have you ever wished for a puppy? _____
7. The count began with ten and went down to zero. _____
8. We shop some of the times that we get together. _____
9. His birth occurred on the last day of June. _____
10. Our collie snatched the ball from the basket. _____
11. Selma wanted cheese on her burger. _____
12. Jill ran out and played on her side of the fence. _____
13. We looked at every part of the frog's body. _____
14. This unusual thing didn't come with any directions. _____
15. A rail fell off the fence and onto the road. _____
16. The pet store sells a special drug to kill fleas. _____
17. Most of the news in our paper is interesting. _____
18. We eat lunch after the clock chimes at noon. _____
19. The end of the week will be here soon. _____

Word Story One of the spelling words was once used to name an evil spirit that sat on the chest of a sleeper. The modern meaning of the word is "a frightening dream." Write the spelling word.

20. _____

Family Tree: *countdown* Think about how the *count* words are alike in spelling and meaning. Then add another *count* word to the tree.

countdown
counted
uncounted
21.
recount
counts
count

Use each spelling word once to complete the story.

The Best Weekend of My Life

It was Sunday, April 7, 1978. I remember the date because my tenth _____ 1 was the day before. I was sitting around, not doing much of _____, when 2 my brother, Gus, walked into the room.

"How would you like to take a ride into Boston with me?" he asked. He pulled out two tickets to the Celtics _____ 3 game. "Happy birthday!"

"I can't believe it!" I screamed. "How did you get those tickets? _____ in 4 Boston wants to see John Havlicek's last game!"

He smiled. "Well, I'd like to say I got them _____ any trouble, but I cannot 5 tell a lie. Waiting _____ the 6 ticket office at the Garden was a real _____. The crowds were 7 unbelievable!"

I ran _____ to get my 8 jacket and raced to the _____ 9 station with Gus. We caught the train that

went into _____ Boston and
            10
arrived a little after noon. All the stores in
the train station and even the little
_____ were filled with
            11
Havlicek buttons. I didn't care much about
eating anything, but Gus bought us each a
big _____, and then
            12
we went _____.
            13

   The Garden was packed with screaming
fans. The crowd was so loud that _____ I couldn't
            14
even hear Gus. Banners hung _____. Some said,
            15
"Boston loves Hondo." That was Havlicek's nickname. When the
speeches were over, Hondo stepped up to the microphone and
said, "Thank you, Boston. I love you!" The fans went wild. It
seemed as though they cheered _____.
            16

   Then the game began. Hondo scored 29 points. A few minutes
before the game ended, he was pulled, and the crowd stood up.
It was the end of a 16-year career. In the last seconds of the game,
the fans began the _____. The Celtics won, but it
            17
was John Havlicek's day. An article in the _____
            18
reported that he turned the lights out in the Garden that night.

   Years have passed since then, but those two days stand out in
my memory. My tenth birthday on Saturday and the Havlicek
game on Sunday _____ made those two days the
            19
best _____ of my life.
     20

Word list (spiral notepad):

basketball
cheeseburger
countdown
newspaper
drugstore
outside
everybody
birthday
upstairs
inside
nightmare
afternoon
anything
forever
sometimes
weekend
downtown
without
everywhere
railroad

Spelling and Writing

basketball
cheeseburger
countdown
newspaper
drugstore
outside
everybody
birthday
upstairs
inside
nightmare
afternoon
anything
forever
sometimes
weekend
downtown
without
everywhere
railroad

Write to the Point

Do you remember a weekend that was one of the best in your life? Write a paragraph about what happened that weekend and what made it so special. Or write about something that you *wish* would happen some weekend. Try to use spelling words from this lesson.

Use the strategies on page 7 when you are not sure how to spell a word.

Proofreading

Proofread the journal entry below. Use proofreading marks to correct five spelling mistakes, two capitalization mistakes, and three punctuation mistakes.

Proofreading Marks

◯ spell correctly
≡ capitalize
⊙ add period

march 10

    I went to Jo's party last weakend. There were

people everywhere. Everebody sang "Happy

Birthday" to Jo Then her mom ran upstares and

brought down a large box withowt a top What do

you think Jo found inside, asleep on some

newspaper? it was a little kitten. Jo had wanted

a kitten more than anything else. I'll remember

the look on her

face fourever

meow

Language Connection

Capital Letters   Geographic names such as names of cities, states, bodies of water, mountains, and streets are capitalized.

> Boston   Utah   Goose Bay
> Swiss Alps   Main Street

The sentences below contain errors in capitalization and spelling. Write each sentence correctly.

1. The <u>Plain Dealer</u> is a noospaper from cleveland, ohio.

2. The rialroad line was built across rollins street.

3. Mr. Diaz spent the aftrnoon fishing on lake erie.

4. We visited niagara falls on my burthday.

5. Would you like to spend the weekind in the rocky mountains?

6. Carly said she wanted to stay in carson city forevr.

⭐ Challenge Yourself

What do you think each Challenge Word means? Check the Spelling Dictionary to see if you are right. Then use separate paper to write sentences showing that you understand the meaning of each Challenge Word.

Challenge Words

farmland
dewdrops
crossroads
dishwasher

7. He loaded the dirty plates and cups into the **dishwasher**.

8. This morning the **dewdrops** on the grass tickled my bare feet.

9. To make driving safer, city workers placed stop signs at the **crossroads**.

10. **Farmland** must have good soil for raising crops.

Abbreviations

1 gal

Say and Listen

Say the spelling word that each abbreviation stands for.

Think and Sort

All of the spelling words are abbreviations. An **abbreviation** is a shortened version of a word. Abbreviations used in street addresses end with a period. Abbreviations of units of measurement and temperature scales do not.

1. Write the **six** abbreviations used in street addresses.

2. Write the **twelve** abbreviations for units of measurement.

3. Write the **two** abbreviations for temperature scales.

1. Street Addresses

2. Units of Measurement

3. Temperature Scales

Ave.
qt
Rd.
cm
F
in
St.
ft
Hwy.
gal
yd
km
l
mi
c
Blvd.
pt
C
m
Rte.

Use the steps on page 6 to study words that are hard for you.

Spelling Patterns

Addresses	Units of Measurement	Temperature Scales
Rte.	qt	C
St.	km	F

Spelling and Meaning

Trading Places Write the abbreviation that can be used instead of the word.

1. Fahrenheit _____
2. gallon _____
3. cup _____
4. yard _____
5. centimeter _____
6. quart _____
7. liter _____
8. Celsius _____
9. pint _____
10. mile _____
11. inch _____
12. kilometer _____
13. foot _____

Clues Write the spelling word for each underlined word.

14. 315 Rose <u>Boulevard</u> _____
15. <u>Route</u> 2, Box 56 _____
16. Box 1010, <u>Highway</u> 47 _____
17. 224 Main <u>Street</u> _____
18. 2067 Green <u>Road</u> _____
19. 1007 Bright <u>Avenue</u> _____

Word Story One spelling word comes from the Greek word *metron,* which meant "a measure or a rule." The spelling word is an abbreviation that means "39.37 inches." Write the abbreviation.

20. _____

Family Tree: *quart* The abbreviation *qt* stands for *quart*. Think about how the *quart* words are alike in spelling and meaning. Then add another *quart* word to the tree.

quarterly

quartet

21. _____

quarts

quart

Use each abbreviation once to complete the selection.

Dear Ming and Lan,

Please make Quick Wheatloaf tonight. You'll need to go to Super Mart and pick up the ingredients. Super Mart is only 5 _____ from
<small>1</small>

our house. (Lan, is this distance equal to 7 or 8 _____? I think
<small>2</small>

you will know the answer, since you just made an A on your measurement

test!) Here are a map and the directions.

North on _____ 25, right onto Lansing _____,
<small>3</small>   <small>4</small>

right onto Circle _____, left on Lakes _____,
<small>5</small>   <small>6</small>

right on Oak _____ Store will be on your left.
<small>7</small>

If you reach the freeway, _____ 12, you've gone too far.
<small>8</small>

You may want to park in the east lot because it's shady. The

east lot is where they had the hundred-_____ dash for
<small>9</small>

free groceries last year.

Raisins are on a high shelf in the store. Ming, you'll need to get the raisins, since you are at least five _____ six
<small>10</small>

_____ tall. Lan can
<small>11</small>

gather the other ingredients.

Love, Mom

P.S. Lan, don't forget to pick

up a _____ of ribbon
<small>12</small>

and a _____ ruler for
<small>13</small>

your math project.

Quick Wheatloaf

Ingredients

1¾ cups whole wheat flour

2 tablespoons wheat germ

½ teaspoon baking soda

pinch of salt

½ cup molasses

½ pint buttermilk or yogurt

½ cup raisins

Mix 1¾ cups flour with wheat germ, baking soda, and salt. Add ½ _____ molasses and ½ _____
           14   **15**

buttermilk to dry ingredients. Stir in raisins. Put dough

into greased loaf pan and bake at 375° _____ or
                                                 16

190° _____ for 30 minutes.
      17

Serving Suggestions For 4 people, serve Quick Wheatloaf

with a _____ of orange juice or milk. This equals a
         18

little more than 1 _____. For more than 4 people,
                 19

serve bread with a _____ of apple cider.
                     20

Ave.
qt
Rd.
cm
F
in
St.
ft
Hwy.
gal
yd
km
l
mi
c
Blvd.
pt
C
m
Rte.

Ave.
qt
Rd.
cm
F
in
St.
ft
Hwy.
gal
yd
km
l
mi
c
Blvd.
pt
C
m
Rte.

Write to the Point

How good are you at giving directions? Can you tell someone how to get to your school or how to make lemonade? Write a list that gives directions telling how to go somewhere or how to prepare a simple snack. Try to use abbreviations from this lesson.

> Use the strategies on page 7 when you are not sure how to spell a word.

Proofreading

Proofread the note below. Use proofreading marks to correct five spelling mistakes, three capitalization mistakes, and two punctuation mistakes.

Proofreading Marks
- ◯ spell correctly
- ≡ capitalize
- ⊙ add period

Kyle,

I have the key to the trunk. You can come by today after school and get it if you want to Here are the directions to my house.

At the corner of Shady Str. and third Av., turn left and go about 50 ft down the block. go past allen Rd and turn right onto Rte. 7. Our house is 1 mle down the road. It is white with blue trim.

The key is under a flower pot about 1 yrd from the mailbox

Ryan

Language Connection

End Punctuation   Three different types of punctuation can be used at the end of a sentence. The period (.) is used for a sentence that tells something or gives commands. The question mark (?) is used for a sentence that asks a question. The exclamation point (!) is used for a sentence that shows excitement or strong feeling.

I like this shirt.	Where are you going?
Move the car, please.	Our team is the greatest!

The sentences below have mistakes in end punctuation and spelling. Write each sentence correctly.

1. My family wants to follow Rt 66 on a vacation

_____

2. Can you tell me how to get to Hway. 12

_____

3. The temperature was 106° Fr in the shade

_____

4. Jessica made 2 gall of lemonade

_____

5. Our family drove 100 mil today

_____

6. The store at 632 Rose Av belongs to my dad

_____

Challenge Yourself

Write the Challenge Word for each clue. Check the Spelling Dictionary to see if you are right. Then use separate paper to write sentences showing that you understand the meaning of each Challenge Word.

Challenge Words	
oz	lb
g	kg

7. My name means one thousand grams. _____

8. I am much less than an ounce. I am used by scientists. _____

9. Most people in the United States use me to tell how much they weigh. _____

10. I am about the same as 28 grams. _____

Words About the Universe

Saturn

1. Two Words

2. One-Syllable Words

3. Two-Syllable Words

4. Three-Syllable Words

5. Four-Syllable Word

rotate
gravity
Jupiter
Pluto
solar system
galaxy
Saturn
universe
Venus
meteor
Earth
satellite
Neptune
comet
Uranus
revolve
Mercury
constellation
Mars
planets

Say and Listen

Say each spelling word. Listen for the number of syllables in each word.

Think and Sort

All of the spelling words are terms that people use to write about the universe. One of the terms contains two words.

1. Write the **one** spelling word that contains two words. Divide each word into syllables.

2. Write the **two** spelling words that have one syllable.

3. Write the **eight** spelling words that have two syllables.

4. Write the **eight** spelling words that have three syllables.

5. Write the **one** spelling word that has four syllables.

Use the steps on page 6 to study words that are hard for you.

Spelling Patterns

One Syllable	Two Syllables	Three Syllables	Four Syllables
Mars	Sat•urn	Ju•pi•ter	con•stel•la•tion

Spelling and Meaning

Clues   Write the spelling word for each clue.

1. planet closest to the sun
2. seventh planet from the sun
3. fourth planet; the "red" one
4. eighth planet; named for the Roman sea god
5. only planet that can support animal life
6. second planet; named for a Roman goddess
7. the planet with "rings"
8. planet farthest from the sun
9. fifth planet from the sun; the largest planet

What's the Answer?   Write a spelling word that answers each question.

10. What moves around the sun and has a long tail?
11. What falls through space toward Earth?
12. What word refers to everything in space?
13. What names a communications object that circles Earth?
14. The Big Dipper is an example of what?
15. Mars, Jupiter, and Venus are examples of what?
16. What do planets do as they travel around the sun?
17. What keeps us from falling off Earth?
18. What does Earth do as it spins on its axis?
19. What are the sun and all the planets called as a group?

Word Story   One spelling word means "a large collection of stars." It comes from *galaxias,* a Greek word meaning "milky." Write the spelling word.

20. _____

Family Tree: *revolve*   Think about how the *revolve* words are alike in spelling and meaning. Then add another *revolve* word to the tree.

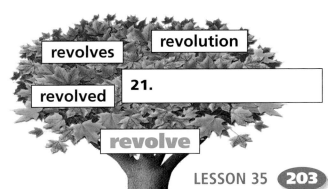

revolves

revolution

revolved

21.

revolve

Use each spelling word once to complete the selection.

The Universe

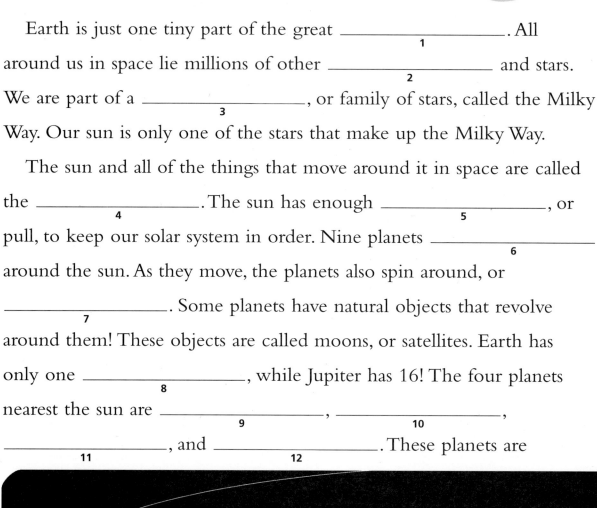

Earth is just one tiny part of the great _____. All
1
around us in space lie millions of other _____ and stars.
2
We are part of a _____, or family of stars, called the Milky
3
Way. Our sun is only one of the stars that make up the Milky Way.

The sun and all of the things that move around it in space are called
the _____. The sun has enough _____, or
4   5
pull, to keep our solar system in order. Nine planets _____
6
around the sun. As they move, the planets also spin around, or
_____. Some planets have natural objects that revolve
7
around them! These objects are called moons, or satellites. Earth has
only one _____, while Jupiter has 16! The four planets
8
nearest the sun are _____, _____,
9   10
_____, and _____. These planets are
11   12

Pluto   Jupiter   Mars   Venu

made mostly of iron and rock. The next four planets are

_____, _____, _____,
13   14   15

and _____. They seem to be made up chiefly of
16

gases. _____ is the farthest planet from the sun.
17

But every 248 years, Pluto moves inside of Neptune's orbit

and becomes the eighth planet for about 20 years. Too little is

known about Pluto to place it in either group of planets.

There are many other interesting parts of the universe.

Star watchers like to pick out groups of stars. A large

_____ called the Big Dipper is a favorite.
18

Others enjoy spotting a shooting star, or _____,
19

blazing through the sky. Some people study the bright tail

of a _____.
20

The universe holds many secrets. As we send off each new

space probe, we come a little closer to understanding what lies

out there in space.

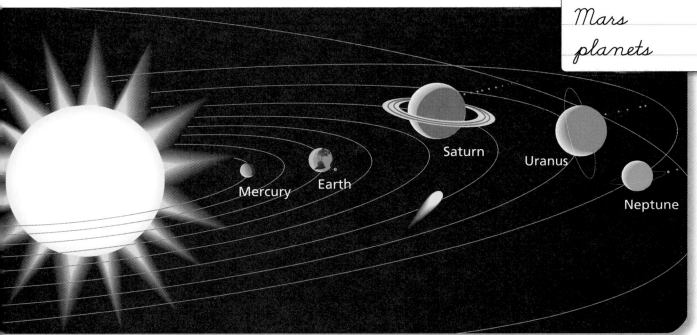

Mercury   Earth   Saturn   Uranus   Neptune

Spelling and Writing

Write to the Point

Have you ever dreamed about traveling in space to visit another planet? Which planet would you visit? What would you take with you to explore it? Write a paragraph about the planet you'd like to explore. Try to use spelling words from this lesson.

Use the strategies on page 7 when you are not sure how to spell a word.

Proofreading

Proofread the following paragraph from a short story. Use proofreading marks to correct five spelling mistakes, two capitalization mistakes, and three missing words.

Proofreading Marks
◯ spell correctly
≡ capitalize
∧ add

After leaving Erth, Captain diego stopped on

Mercurie, venus, and Mars. He had a close call when a

metiore almost hit the spaceship. When we last heard

from him, he heading for Pluto, at the

far edge our solor system. He plans see

the whole galaxy, maybe even

the uneverse.

rotate
gravity
Jupiter
Pluto
solar system
galaxy
Saturn
universe
Venus
meteor
Earth
satellite
Neptune
comet
Uranus
revolve
Mercury
constellation
Mars
planets

Using the Spelling Table

A spelling table can help you find the spelling of a word in a dictionary. Suppose you are not sure how the first vowel sound in *comet* is spelled. You can use a spelling table to find the different spellings for the sound. First, find the pronunciation symbol for the sound. Then read the first spelling listed for /ŏ/, and look up *ca* in the dictionary. Look for each spelling in the dictionary until you find the correct one.

Sound	Spellings	Examples
/ŏ/	o a	doctor, wash

Write the correct spelling for each word. Use the Spelling Table on page 213 and the Spelling Dictionary.

1. klĕnz _____

2. hōst _____

3. pēch _____

4. hôrd _____

5. **lär′** və _____

6. **bûr′** glər _____

7. skwŏd _____

8. bō **kā′** _____

 ## Challenge Yourself

Use the Spelling Dictionary to answer these questions. Then use separate paper to write sentences showing that you understand the meaning of each Challenge Word.

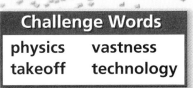

Challenge Words

physics   vastness
takeoff   technology

9. Is it important to understand **physics** before

   you start to build a spaceship? _____

10. Can we explore the **vastness** of outer space in one day?

    _____

11. If a rocket is ready for **takeoff**, is it ready to land?

    _____

12. Without **technology**, could people walk on the moon?

    _____

Unit 6 Review
Lessons 31–35

Use the steps on page 6 to study words that are hard for you.

31

circle
early
world
germ
clear
here
period
cheer

Words with /ûr/ or /îr/

Write the spelling word that belongs in each group.

1. Earth, globe, _____
2. bug, virus, _____
3. beginning, first, _____
4. square, triangle, _____
5. at this place, in this spot, _____
6. shout, yell, _____
7. comma, hyphen, _____
8. obvious, plain, _____

32

whether
special
automobile
animal
wrinkle

Words with /ə/

Write the spelling word that completes each analogy.

9. *Drive* is to _____ as *fly* is to *plane*.
10. *Though* is to *however* as _____ is to *if*.
11. *Garden* is to *flower* as *zoo* is to _____.
12. *Crease* is to _____ as *flat* is to *level*.
13. *Unique* is to *common* as _____ is to *ordinary*.

33

without
everywhere
birthday

Compound Words

Write the spelling word that completes each sentence.

14. If you don't have any assignments, you are
   _____ homework.

15. When something is in all places, it is
   _____.

16. When you become a year older, you celebrate
   your _____.

Blvd.
in
gal
cm
F

Abbreviations

Write the spelling word that is the abbreviation for the underlined word in each phrase.

17. 12 <u>inches</u>   _____

18. 98° <u>Fahrenheit</u>   _____

19. 631 River <u>Boulevard</u>   _____

20. 3 <u>gallons</u>   _____

21. 5 <u>centimeters</u>   _____

Mercury
satellite
gravity
constellation

Words About the Universe

Write the spelling word for each definition.

22. a heavenly body that revolves around a planet

_____

23. the force that causes objects to move toward the center of the earth   _____

24. the planet closest to the sun   _____

25. a group of stars with a recognizable shape

_____

26. Compound Words

_____

_____

_____

27. /ûr/ Words

_____

_____

_____

28. /îr/ Words

_____

_____

_____

_____

29. /ə/ Words

_____

_____

_____

_____

_____

30. Abbreviations

_____

_____

_____

_____

_____

Review Sort

clear	wrinkle	cm	animal
F	everywhere	special	birthday
germ	gal	circle	here
in	without	Blvd.	whether
early	cheer	automobile	

26. Write the **three** spelling words that are made up of two shorter words.

27. Write the **three** spelling words with /ûr/. Circle the letters that spell /ûr/ in each word.

28. Write the **four** spelling words with /îr/. Circle the letters that spell /îr/ in each word.

29. Write the **five** spelling words with /ə/. Circle the letter or letters that spell /ə/ in each word.

30. Write the **five** abbreviations.

These four words have been sorted into two groups. Explain how the words in each group are alike.

31. Venus   Pluto

_____

_____

32. Mercury   Jupiter

_____

_____

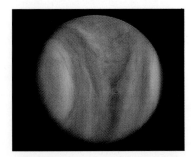

Writer's Workshop

A Description

A description of a person is often called a character sketch. In a character sketch, the writer describes how a person acts and looks. The writer concentrates on the things that stand out most about the person. Here is the beginning of Sheila's description of her brother, Dom. What things about Sheila's brother stand out most?

Prewriting To write her description, Sheila followed the steps in the writing process. After she decided which person to describe, she made a list of details that she could use to describe her brother. The list helped Sheila decide which details to include in her description. Part of Sheila's list is shown here. Study what Sheila did.

Dom

My brother, Dom, is eleven years old, but people usually think he is older because he is very tall for his age. He has short black hair that is very curly. He likes to wear my dad's old sweatshirts.

Dom is a very cheerful person. He is always smiling and laughing, and he makes other people laugh.

My brother Dom
how he looks
  tall
  curly black hair
  wears sweatshirts
  has freckles
how he acts
  cheerful
  friendly

It's Your Turn!

Write your own description of a person. You can write about someone in your neighborhood, your school, or anyone you wish. After you have decided on your topic, make a list. Then follow the other steps in the writing process—writing, revising, proofreading, and publishing. Try to use spelling words from this lesson in your description.

Commonly Misspelled Words

about	every	myself	they
above	family	name	they're
across	favorite	nice	though
again	finally	now	through
a lot	first	once	today
always	friend	other	together
another	get	outside	tomorrow
beautiful	getting	party	too
because	goes	people	two
been	guess	play	until
before	happened	please	upon
beginning	have	pretty	very
believe	hear	read	want
birthday	here	really	went
bought	hospital	right	were
buy	house	said	we're
came	into	saw	when
children	it's	scared	where
come	know	school	with
cousin	little	sent	would
didn't	made	some	write
different	make	sometimes	writing
does	many	swimming	wrote
doesn't	might	their	your
enough	morning	there	you're

Spelling Table

Sound	Spellings	Examples
/ă/	a ai au	match, plaid, laugh
/ā/	a a_e ai ay ea ei eigh ey	April, chase, plain, day, break, reign, eight, obey
/ä/	a	father
/âr/	air are eir ere ey're	fair, share, their, there, they're
/b/	b bb	bus, rabbit
/ch/	ch tch t	child, match, picture
/d/	d dd	dish, address
/ĕ/	e ea ie ai ue	never, bread, friend, again, guess
/ē/	e e_e ea ee ei eo ey i i_e ie y	zebra, these, please, sweet, deceive, people, key, ski, police, cities, city
/f/	f ff gh	feet, offer, laugh
/g/	g gg	go, jogging
/h/	h wh	hope, who
/ĭ/	i a e ee u ui y	quick, package, secret, been, busy, building, gym
/ī/	i i_e ie igh eye uy y	child, life, die, night, eyesight, buy, dry
/îr/	er ear eer eir ere	period, hear, cheer, weird, here
/j/	j g dg	jog, tragic, edge
/k/	k c ck ch	keep, coast, package, chorus
/ks/	x	axle
/kw/	qu	squeeze
/l/	l ll	life, balloon
/m/	m mb mm	man, comb, swimming

Sound	Spellings	Examples
/n/	n kn nn	nose, knot, beginning
/ng/	n ng	monkey, anything
/ŏ/	o a	doctor, wash
/ō/	o o_e oa oe ow ou ough	zero, those, coach, toe, hollow, boulder, though
/oi/	oi oy	coin, royal
/ô/	o a au augh aw ough	strong, already, cause, taught, shawl, bought
/o͝o/	oo o ou u	wool, wolf, could, full
/o͞o/	oo ew u u_e ue ui o ou	shoot, grew, truly, tune, blue, fruit, two, soup
/ou/	ou ow	ours, towel
/p/	p pp	pay, happen
/r/	r rr wr	reply, hurry, wrinkle
/s/	s ss c	save, pass, fence
/sh/	sh s ce	shape, sugar, ocean
/t/	t tt ed	taste, button, thanked
/th/	th	that
/th/	th	thick
/ŭ/	u o o_e oe oo ou	brush, month, become, does, blood, touch
/ûr/	ur ir er ear ere or our	curve, third, germ, earn, were, world, flourish
/v/	v f	voice, of
/w/	w wh o	win, where, once
/y/	y	yawn
/yo͞o/	u_e ew eau	use, new, beautiful
/z/	z zz s	zebra, blizzard, trees
/ə/	a e i o u	special, often, family, together, surprise

Spelling Dictionary

Major Parts of a Dictionary Entry

The **pronunciation** tells how to pronounce the word.

The **parts of speech** are identified by abbreviations.

The **entry word** is divided into syllables.

One or more **definitions** tell you what the word means.

show·er (shou′ ər) *n.* **1.** A short fall of rain. **2.** A steady flow of something: *a shower of gifts.* **3.** A shower bath. **4.** A party to honor someone: *a baby shower.* —*v.* **show·ered, show·er·ing. 1.** To fall down as in a shower. **2.** To bestow: *The grandparents showered the baby with love.*

Other **major forms** of a verb are given. The plural form of nouns is sometimes given.

A **sample sentence or phrase** helps to make the meaning clear.

---

a·bove (ə bŭv′) *adv.* In a higher place: *The sun shone above.* —*prep.* Over; higher than: *a bird above the clouds.*

ab·sence (ăb′ səns) *n.* The condition of not being present: *Your absence from school was noticed.*

ac·cuse (ə kyōōz′) *v.* **ac·cused, ac·cus·ing.** To blame someone for doing something wrong: *Did Marcus accuse him of breaking the window?*

ac·knowl·edge (ăk nŏl′ ĭj) *v.* **ac·knowl·edged, ac·knowl·edg·ing.** To admit as true or as existing: *I acknowledge that I was wrong.*

ac·quaint (ə kwānt′) *v.* **ac·quaint·ed, ac·quaint·ing.** To make or become familiar: *I must acquaint myself with the rules of the game.*

ac·quire (ə kwīr′) *v.* **ac·quired, ac·quir·ing.** To get or gain: *How did you acquire that baseball card?*

ac·ro·bat (ăk′ rə băt′) *n.* A person who is skilled in performing daring actions such as swinging on a trapeze or walking a tightrope.

ad·dress (ə drĕs′) *n. also* **(ăd′ rĕs′).** The place where a person lives, works, or gets mail. —*v.* **ad·dressed, ad·dress·ing. 1.** To write on mail where it should go. **2.** To speak to: *address a crowd.*

a·dorn (ə dôrn′) *v.* **a·dorned, a·dorn·ing.** To decorate in order to make beautiful.

a·fraid (ə frād′) *adj.* **1.** Fearful; frightened: *afraid of high places.* **2.** Sorry to say: *I'm afraid you're right.*

af·ter·noon (ăf′ tər nōōn′) *n.* The part of the day between noon and sunset.

a·gain (ə gĕn′) *adv.* **1.** Once more: *Let me try again.* **2.** On the other hand: *It may snow, and again it may not.*

a·gainst (ə gĕnst′) *prep.* **1.** In a position opposite to: *against the rules.* **2.** So as to meet: *He hit the ball against the wall.*

air (âr) *n.* The mixture of gases surrounding the earth.

air·borne (âr′ bôrn′) *adj.* **1.** Carried by or through the air: *an airborne leaf.* **2.** Flying: *The plane is now airborne.*

a·larm (ə lärm′) *n.* **1.** Sudden fear of danger: *cause for alarm.* **2.** A signal to warn people: *a fire alarm.* —*v.* **a·larmed, a·larm·ing.** To frighten.

al·most (ôl′ mōst) *or* (ôl mōst′) *adv.* Just about; nearly: *The pie is almost ready.*

a·lone (ə lōn′) *adj.* Without the company of other people or things. —*adv.* Without help: *I cooked dinner alone.*

al·read·y (ôl rĕd′ ē) *adv.* By this time: *The book is already overdue.*

a·mong (ə mŭng′) *prep.* **1.** One of: *Monkeys are among the best-loved animals.* **2.** In the company of: *among relatives.* **3.** With portions to each: *divided among us.*

an·gry (ăng′ grē) *adj.* **an·gri·er, an·gri·est.** Feeling or showing anger: *an angry neighbor; an angry look.*

an·i·mal (ăn′ ə məl) *n.* A living thing differing from a plant by its ability to move about, grow to a limited size and shape, and feed upon other animals or plants.

an·oth·er (ə nŭth′ ər) *adj.* **1.** Different: *another way to go.* **2.** One more: *another piece of pie.*

an·swer (ăn′ sər) *n.* **1.** A spoken or written response to a question. **2.** Solution to a problem. —*v.* **an·swered, an·swer·ing.** To reply.

an·y·thing (ĕn′ ē thĭng′) *pron.* Any object, event, or subject whatever.

a·part (ə pärt′) *adv.* **1.** Separate in time or distance: *lived apart.* **2.** In pieces: *The toy fell apart.*

ap·plaud (ə plôd′) *v.* **ap·plaud·ed, ap·plaud·ing.** To clap hands to show approval: *The Senate did not applaud the President's speech.*

ap·point (ə point′) *v.* **ap·point·ed, ap·point·ing.** To name or choose for a duty or position: *The teacher will appoint the class helpers.*

Pronunciation Key

ă	pat	ŏ	pot	ŭ	cut
ā	pay	ō	toe	ûr	urge
âr	care	ô	paw, for	ə	about,
ä	father	oi	noise		item,
ĕ	pet	ŏŏ	took		edible,
ē	bee	ōō	boot		gallop,
ĭ	pit	ou	out		circus
ī	pie	th	thin	ər	butter
îr	deer	*th*	*th*is		

ap·pro·pri·ate (ə prō′ prē ĭt) *adj.* Right; proper: *Games are appropriate gifts for a ten-year-old.*

a·pri·cot (ăp′ rĭ kŏt′) *or* (ā′ prĭ kŏt′) *n.* A juicy, round, yellowish-orange fruit that looks like a peach.

A·pril (ā′ prəl) *n.* The fourth month of the year.

aren't (ärnt) *or* (är′ ənt) **1.** Contraction of **are not.** **2.** Contraction of **am not** (in questions).

ask (ăsk) *v.* **asked, ask·ing. 1.** To question: *She asked him about his house.* **2.** To request: *Ask him to sing!* **3.** To invite: *She asked them to dinner.*

at·tor·ney (ə tûr′ nē) *n., pl.* **at·tor·neys.** A lawyer.

auc·tion (ôk′ shən) *n.* A public sale at which things are sold to the people who offer the most money: *The movie star's car will be sold at an auction.* —*v.* **auc·tioned, auc·tion·ing.** To sell at an auction: *The museum will auction the painting.*

au·di·o (ô′ dē ō′) *adj.* Having to do with sound or how it is recorded, played, or received: *New audio equipment will make the band concerts sound better.*

Au·gust (ô′ gəst) *n.* The eighth month of the year.

aunt (ănt) *or* (änt) *n.* **1.** The sister of one's father or mother. **2.** The wife of one's uncle.

au·thor (ô′ thər) *n.* A person who writes books, stories, etc.

au·to·mo·bile (ô′ tə mō **bēl′**) or (-**mō′** bēl′) or (**ô′** tə mə bēl′) n. A passenger vehicle for use on land. It carries its own engine and moves on four wheels.

au·tumn (ô′ təm) n. The season of the year between summer and winter; fall.

Ave. Abbreviation of **Avenue.**

a·void (ə **void′**) v. **a·void·ed, a·void·ing.** **1.** To keep away from: *avoid traffic.* **2.** To prevent: *avoid catching cold.*

a·wake (ə **wāk′**) v. **a·woke** or **a·waked, a·wak·ing.** To rise from sleep. —*adj.* Not asleep: *Rita was wide awake.*

awe·some (ô′ səm) adj. Causing wonder, respect, or fear: *The Grand Canyon is an awesome sight.*

a·while (ə **wīl′**) adv. For a short time: *They sat awhile.*

ax·le (**ăk′** səl) n. A bar on which a wheel or set of wheels turns: *A car cannot go if its axle is broken.*

ba·by (**bā′** bē) n., pl. **ba·bies.** **1.** A very young child; infant. **2.** The youngest in a group or family.

bal·loon (bə **loon′**) n. **1.** An airtight bag filled with gas that is lighter than air so that it will float. **2.** A child's toy made of plastic or rubber and filled with air.

ba·nan·a (bə **năn′** ə) n. A crescent-shaped tropical fruit that is sweet, soft, and yellow-skinned.

ban·ish (**băn′** ĭsh) v. **ban·ished, ban·ish·ing.** To force to leave a country or place: *The king will banish the robbers.*

bar·ri·er (**băr′** ē ər) n. Something that blocks the way or blocks movement: *The fallen tree formed a barrier on the road.*

bas·ket·ball (**băs′** kĭt bôl′) n. **1.** A game played by two teams. Players toss a ball through a basket defended by another team. **2.** The ball used in this game.

beach (bēch) n. The shore beside a body of water.

bea·con (**bē′** kən) n. A light or other type of signal that guides or warns: *The beacon guided the ship to the dock.*

beau·ti·ful (**byoo′**tə fəl) adj. Having beauty; pleasing to see or hear: *the beautiful gem.*

be·cause (bĭ **kôz′**) or (-**kŭz′**) conj. For the reason that: *He went to bed because he was tired.*

be·come (bĭ **kŭm′**) v. **be·came, be·come, be·com·ing.** To grow to be: *become restless.*

be·fore (bĭ **fôr′**) adv. Earlier: *I've been here before.* —*prep.* Earlier than: *She woke up before me.*

be·gan Look up **begin.**

be·gin (bĭ **gĭn′**) v. **be·gan** (bĭ **găn′**), **be·gun, be·gin·ning. 1.** To start. **2.** Come or bring into being: *The storm began an hour ago.*

be·gin·ning (bĭ **gĭn′** ĭng) n. The start; the first part.

be·hind (bĭ **hīnd′**) prep. In back of: *He hid behind the chair.*

be·low (bĭ **lō′**) adv. Lower than; under: *The playroom is below the living room.*

be·side (bĭ **sīd′**) prep. At the side of: *The house stood beside the lake.*

be·tray (bĭ **trā′**) v. **be·trayed, be·tray·ing. 1.** To help the enemy of: *The man would not betray his country.* **2.** To be disloyal to.

be·tween (bĭ **twēn′**) prep. In the time or space separating two things: *The river runs between Texas and Mexico.*

be·yond (bē **ŏnd′**) or (bĭ **yŏnd′**) prep. On the farther side of: *His paper route goes beyond the school.*

bin·oc·u·lars (bə **nŏk′** yə lərz) or (-**bī**) n. A device consisting of two small telescopes joined together that makes distant objects look closer and larger: *We used binoculars to see the eagle's nest.*

birth (bûrth) n. The beginning of existence: *the birth of the baby.*

birth·day (bûrth′ dā′) *n.* **1.** The day on which a person is born. **2.** The yearly return of that day.

blind (blīnd) *adj.* **blind·er, blind·est 1.** Unable to see: *a blind person.* **2.** Hidden: *a blind curve.* —*v.* To make unable to see: *The bright light blinded him.*

bliz·zard (blĭz′ ərd) *n.* A heavy snowstorm with strong winds.

blood (blŭd) *n.* Red liquid circulated through the body by the heart, carrying oxygen and food to body parts.

blouse (blous) *or* (blouz) *n.* A loose shirtlike piece of clothing for the part of the body from the neck to waist: *Yesterday Ling wore a blue blouse.*

Blvd. Abbreviation of **Boulevard.**

bod·y (bŏd′ ē) *n., pl.* **bod·ies.** The whole physical structure of a living thing: *I jog to keep my body in shape.*

book·store (bŏŏk′ stôr′) *or* (-stōr′) *n.* A store that sells books.

boost (bŏŏst) *n.* A shove or push upward: *Give me a boost over the fence.*

bot·tom (bŏt′ əm) *n.* The lowest part of anything: *The bottom of the barrel.*

bought Look up **buy.**

bou·quet (bō kā′) *or* (bŏŏ-) *n.* A number of flowers grouped together: *Mom received a beautiful bouquet of tulips.*

box (bŏks) *n. pl.* **box·es.** A container having four sides, a bottom, and a lid.

branch (brănch) *n., pl.* **branch·es.** A woody stem growing out from the trunk of a tree.

bread (brĕd) *n.* A food made from flour or meal.

break (brāk) *v.* **broke** (brōk), **bro·ken, break·ing. 1.** To come apart; split into fragments. **2.** To make unusable: *Adam broke my radio.*

break·fast (brĕk′ fəst) *n.* The first meal of the day: *It is always important to eat a good breakfast.*

Pronunciation Key

ă	pat	ŏ	pot	ŭ	cut
ā	pay	ō	toe	ûr	urge
âr	care	ô	paw, for	ə	about,
ä	father	oi	noise		item,
ĕ	pet	ŏŏ	took		edible,
ē	bee	ōō	boot		gallop,
ĭ	pit	ou	out		circus
ī	pie	th	thin	ər	butter
îr	deer	*th*	**th**is		

bridge (brĭj) *n.* A structure built over a river, railroad, or other obstacle, providing a way across.

bright (brīt) *adj.* **bright·er, bright·est. 1.** Giving off light in large amounts: *the bright sun.* **2.** Smart: *a bright child.*

bring (brĭng) *v.* **brought** (brôt), **bring·ing.** To carry along: *Bring some pajamas with you!*

broke Look up **break.**

brook (brŏŏk) *n.* A small freshwater stream.

broth·er (brŭ*th*′ ər) *n., pl.* **broth·ers.** A boy or man whose parents are the same as another person's.

brought Look up **bring.**

brush (brŭsh) *n., pl.* **brush·es.** A tool with bristles used for cleaning, painting, grooming, etc. —*v.* **brushed, brush·ing. 1.** To clean, paint, or groom with a brush. **2.** To touch in passing.

build·ing (bĭl′ dĭng) *n.* **1.** Something that is built: *an apartment building.* **2.** The process of constructing.

bur·glar (bûr′ glər) *n., pl.* **bur·glars.** A person who breaks into a house, store, or other building to steal something.

bus (bŭs) *n., pl.* **bus·es.** A large motor vehicle equipped to carry many passengers.

bush (bŏŏsh) *n.* A small, woody, branching plant: *I love the smell of our lilac bush!*

bus·y (bĭz′ ē) *adj.* **bus·i·er, bus·i·est.** Having a lot to do; active: *the busy secretary.*

but·ton (bŭt′ n) *n.* A small disk sewn to clothes to hold them closed or decorate them.

buy (bī) *v.* **bought** (bôt), **buy·ing.** To get in exchange for money; purchase: *I would love to buy that desk. These sound alike:* **buy, by.**

C Abbreviation of **Celsius.**

c Abbreviation of **cup.**

cal·en·dar (kăl′ ən dər) *n.* A table showing time by days, weeks, months, and years.

can (kăn) *or* (kən) *aux. v.* **could** (kŏŏd) *or* (kəd). Able to do or accomplish: *I can ride a bike.*

Can·a·da (kăn′ ə də) *n.* A North American country extending from the Atlantic to the Pacific and from the United States to the Arctic Ocean.

care·ful (kâr′ fəl) *adj.* **1.** Taking care; watchful. **2.** Done with care.

car·ry (kăr′ ē) *v.* **car·ried, car·ry·ing.** To hold in the hands or on the back while moving.

car·toon (kär tōōn′) *n.* **1.** A drawing showing people, things, or events in a humorous way. **2.** A comic strip. **3.** An animated film.

catch (kăch) *or* (kĕch) *v.* **caught** (kôt), **catch·ing. 1.** To grab hold of: *catch the ball.* **2.** To trap: *We set traps to catch the mice.*

caught Look up **catch.**

cause (kôz) *n.* **1.** The person or thing that makes something happen. **2.** The reason for an action. —*v.* **caused, caus·ing.** To make happen: *Carelessness caused the fire.*

change (chānj) *v.* **changed, chang·ing. 1.** To make or become different. **2.** To put in place of another. **3.** To exchange.

chap·ter (chăp′ tər) *n.* A main division of a book: *the chapter on trout fishing.*

chase (chās) *v.* **chased, chas·ing. 1.** To run after or follow in order to catch. **2.** To drive away.

cheer (chîr) *v.* **cheered, cheer·ing. 1.** To shout in praise. **2.** To give support: *The team cheered her on!*

cheese·burg·er (chēz′ bûr′ gər) *n.* A hamburger topped with melted cheese.

chick·en (chĭk′ ən) *n.* Domestic fowl raised for food; hen or rooster.

child (chīld) *n., pl.* **chil·dren** (chĭl′ drən). **1.** A young boy or young girl. **2.** A son or daughter.

chil·dren Look up **child.**

choice (chois) *n.* **1.** The act of choosing or selecting. **2.** A person or thing chosen.

choose (chōōz) *v.* **chose** (chōz), **cho·sen, choos·ing. 1.** To select from a number; pick out. **2.** To decide: *He chose to stay inside.*

cho·rus (kôr′ əs) *n.* A group of singers who perform all together.
   Idiom. **in chorus.** In unison.

chose Look up **choose.**

cir·cle (sûr′ kəl) *n.* A closed curve with all points equally distant from its fixed center.

cir·cus (sûr′ kəs) *n.* A show with acrobats, clowns, and trained animals.

cit·y (sĭt′ ē) *n., pl.* **cit·ies.** A center of people, business, and culture; an important town.

class (klăs) *n., pl.* **class·es. 1.** A set of people or things alike in some way. **2.** A group of students learning together.

cleanse (klĕnz) *v.* **cleansed, cleans·ing.** To make clean: *The doctor will cleanse the cut.*

clear (klîr) *adj.* **clear·er, clear·est. 1.** Free from haze, mist, clouds. **2.** Easily seen, heard, or understood. **3.** Plain, evident.

climb (klīm) *v.* **climbed, climb·ing. 1.** To go up by using hands or feet. **2.** To rise.

close (klōs) *adj.* **clos·er, clos·est.** Near; together in time or space. —*v.* (klōz) **closed, clos·ing.** To shut: *Close the door. These sound alike:* **close, clothes.**

clothes (klōz) *or* (klō*th*z) *n.* Coverings for a person's body. *These sound alike:* **clothes, close.**

cloud (kloud) *n.* **1.** A mass of water droplets or ice particles in the air.

cm Abbreviation for **centimeter.**

coach (kōch) *n.* **1.** A large carriage pulled by horses. **2.** A railroad passenger car. **3.** A person who trains athletic teams.

coast (kōst) *n.* The land along the sea.

cof•fee (kô′ fē) *or* (kŏf′ ē) *n.* A brown drink made from ground, roasted seeds of a tropical tree.

coin (koin) *n.* A piece of flat metal stamped by the government and used as money.

col•lage (kə läzh′) *n.* A picture made by pasting different kinds of materials or objects on a surface: *I made a collage of newspaper, yarn, and bottle caps for my art project.*

col•lide (kə līd′) *v.* **col•lid•ed, col•lid•ing.** To crash against each other with force: *We saw the cars collide on the highway.*

comb (kōm) *n.* A piece of metal, plastic, etc. with teeth used to arrange hair. —*v.* **combed, comb•ing. 1.** To arrange with a comb. **2.** To search.

com•et (kŏm′ ĭt) *n.* A bright solar system object with a starlike center and a tail of light.

con•ceal (kən sēl′) *v.* **con•cealed, con•ceal•ing.** To keep someone or something out of sight or unknown; hide: *She tried to conceal her anger.*

con•stel•la•tion (kŏn′ stə lā′ shən) *n.* A group of stars having a recognized shape: *The Big Dipper is a familiar constellation.*

con•struct (kən strŭkt′) *v.* **con•struct•ed, con•struct•ing.** To build by putting parts together: *The class will construct a model airport.*

con•test (kŏn′ tĕst′) *n.* **1.** A fight or struggle. **2.** A competition rated by judges: *an ice-skating contest.*

con•trib•ute (kən trĭb′ yo͞ot) *v.* **con•trib•ut•ed, con•trib•ut•ing.** To give along with others: *Tom will contribute money to help the flood victims.*

con•vert (kən vûrt′) *v.* **con•vert•ed, con•vert•ing.** To change a thing into something different or into another form: *convert snow into water.*

cook (ko͝ok) *v.* **cooked, cook•ing.** To prepare food by using heat.

cop•y (kŏp′ ē) *n., pl.* **cop•ies.** A thing made to be exactly like another. —*v.* **cop•ied, cop•y•ing.** To follow as a model; imitate.

cot•ton (kŏt′ n) *n.* **1.** A plant with soft white fibers surrounding the seeds. **2.** Cloth made from these fibers.

Pronunciation Key

ă	pat	ŏ	pot	ŭ	cut
ā	pay	ō	toe	ûr	urge
âr	care	ô	paw, for	ə	about,
ä	father	oi	noise		item,
ĕ	pet	o͝o	took		edible,
ē	bee	o͞o	boot		gallop,
ĭ	pit	ou	out		circus
ī	pie	th	thin	ər	butter
îr	deer	*th*	this		

cou•gar (ko͞o′gər) *n.* A large brown cat also called mountain lion.

could Look up **can.**

could•n't (ko͝od′ nt) Contraction of **could not.**

coun•sel•or (koun′ sə lər) *or* (koun′ slər) *n.* A person who gives advice or helps: *a school counselor.*

count•down (kount′ doun′) *n.* The process of counting time backward until the time a special event is to take place.

count•er (koun′ tər) *n.* A narrow table on which money is counted or food is served.

coun•try (kŭn′ trē) *n., pl.* **coun•tries. 1.** A nation. **2.** Land; a region: *rough, rocky country.*

coun•try•side (kŭn′ trē sīd′) *n.* The region outside towns and cities: *In the countryside we saw rolling fields and tall trees.*

cou•ple (kŭp′ əl) *n.* **1.** Two things of the same kind. **2.** A man and woman who are married; partners. **3.** A few.

cou•pon (ko͞o′ pŏn′) *or* (kyo͞o′-) *n.* A ticket or form that can be exchanged to save money or to get something: *I had a coupon for the movie.*

cour•te•sy (kûr′ tĭ sē) *n., pl.* **cour•te•sies.** Behavior that shows good manners and thoughtfulness; politeness: *It is a courtesy to say "thank you" for a gift.*

cov•er (kŭv′ ər) *v.* **cov•ered, cov•er•ing. 1.** To place something over. **2.** To occupy the surface of.

crack (krăk) *n.* **1.** A sharp, snapping sound. **2.** A narrow space.

crawl (krôl) *v.* **crawled, crawl·ing.** To move slowly by dragging oneself.

cried Look up **cry.**

cross·roads (krôs′ rōds′) *or* (krŏs′-) *n.* (*used with a singular verb*). A place where two or more roads meet or cross, often in the countryside: *The crossroads is a busy place.*

crowd (kroud) *n.* A large number of people together.

crowd·ed (kroud′ ĭd) *adj.* Filled to excess; packed.

crown (kroun) *n.* A head covering of metal and jewels worn by a king or queen.

cry (krī) *v.* **cried, cry·ing, cries. 1.** To shed tears; weep. **2.** To call out loudly; shout.

curve (kûrv) *n.* A line that has no straight part and is smooth and continuous.

cus·tom·ar·y (kŭs′ tə mĕr′ ē) *adj.* Commonly done; usual: *It is customary to eat dessert last.*

daugh·ter (dô′ tər) *n.* A female child or offspring.

dawn (dôn) *n.* The beginning of day; first appearance of daylight.

deaf·en (dĕf′ ən) *v.* **deaf·ened, deaf·en·ing.** To make unable to hear: *Music played too loudly can deafen a person.*

dear (dîr) *adj.* **dear·er, dear·est.** Loved; precious: *my dear sister. These sound alike:* **dear, deer.**

De·cem·ber (dĭ sĕm′ bər) *n.* The twelfth month of the year.

de·fi·ant (dĭ fī′ ənt) *adj.* Showing that one will not obey or respect something or someone in control: *The defiant child would not go to bed.*

de·liv·er (dĭ lĭv′ ər) *v.* **de·liv·ered, de·liv·er·ing.** To carry or take to a person to whom something is addressed: *deliver mail.*

de·ny (dĭ nī′) *v.* **de·nied, de·ny·ing, de·nies.** To declare something untrue: *deny a rumor.*

des·ert¹ (dĕz′ ərt) *n.* A dry region that is sandy and without trees.

de·sert² (dĭ zûrt′) *v.* **de·sert·ed, de·sert·ing.** To leave: *desert the sinking ship.*

de·stroy (dĭ stroi′) *v.* **de·stroyed, de·stroy·ing. 1.** To ruin or spoil; make useless. **2.** To put an end to: *destroy their dream.*

dew·drop (dōō′ drŏp′) *or* (dyōō′-) *n., pl.* **dew·drops.** A drop of water from the air that collects on cool surfaces, usually at night: *The dewdrops sparkled on the grass.*

did·n't (dĭd′ nt) Contraction of **did not.**

die (dī) *v.* **died, dy·ing. 1.** To stop living. **2.** To lose strength: *The wind died down. These sound alike:* **die, dye.**

dif·fer·ent (dĭf′ ər ənt) *or* (dĭf′ rənt) *adj.* **1.** Not alike: *A car is different from a plane.* **2.** Separate: *three different men.*

dig·ni·fy (dĭg′ nə fī′) *v.* **dig·ni·fied, dig·ni·fy·ing.** To give honor to: *It was kind of the teacher to dignify his question with a long answer.*

di·no·saur (dī′ nə sôr′) *n.* Any one of a group of extinct reptiles that inhabited the earth millions of years ago.

dirt·y (dûr′ tē) *adj.* **dirt·i·er, dirt·i·est.** Not clean; soiled: *dirty laundry.*

dis·cov·er (dĭ skŭv′ ər) *v.* **dis·cov·ered, dis·cov·er·ing.** To find out through study or observation: *discover a new medicine.*

dish (dĭsh) *n., pl.* **dish·es. 1.** A flat container for serving food. **2.** Food served: *Ice cream is a tasty dish.*

dish·wash·er (dĭsh′ wŏsh′ ər) *or* (dĭsh′ wô′ shər) *n.* **1.** A machine that is used for washing dishes. **2.** A person who washes dishes.

dis·mal (dĭz′ məl) *adj.* Causing, feeling, or showing sadness or gloom: *The cold, rainy day was dismal.*

dis·pose (dĭ spōz′) *v.* **dis·posed, dis·pos·ing.** To arrange. *Idiom.* **dispose of. 1.** To settle. **2.** To get rid of.

do (dōō) *v.* **did, done** (dŭn), **do·ing, does** (dŭz). To cause to happen; carry out; perform. —*aux. v.* **1.** Used to ask questions: *Do you have a problem?* **2.** Used to make negative statements: *I did not want any milk.*

doc·tor (dŏk′ tər) *n.* A person trained and licensed to practice medicine.

does Look up **do.**

does·n't (dŭz′ ənt) Contraction of **does not.**

dol·lar (dŏl′ ər) *n.* Basic unit of money in the United States and Canada, equal to 100 cents.

done (dŭn) —*adj.* **1.** Finished or completed: *Her work is done.* **2.** Cooked: *well-done meat.*

don't (dōnt) Contraction of **do not.**

dou·ble (dŭb′ əl) *adj.* **1.** Twice as much as. **2.** Made up of two like parts: *a double dresser.*

down·town (doun′ toun′) *adj.* Being in the center or main business section of a city.

Dr. Abbreviation of **doctor.**

drap·er·y (drā′ pə rē) *n.,* *pl.* **drap·er·ies.** Long, heavy curtains that hang in loose folds.

drows·y (drou′ zē) *adj.* **drows·i·er, drows·i·est.** Sleepy: *I felt drowsy after the big dinner.*

drug·store (drŭg′ stôr′) *n.* A store where prescriptions are filled.

dry (drī) *adj.* **dri·er** or **dry·er, dri·est** or **dry·est.** Not wet or damp: *A desert is dry.* —*v.* **dried, dry·ing.** To make or become dry: *She dried the dishes.*

dur·ing (dŏŏr′ ĭng) *or* (dyŏŏr′-) *prep.* Throughout the course of: *Bears hibernate during winter.*

dwin·dle (dwĭn′ dəl) *v.* **dwin·dled, dwin·dling.** To gradually become less or smaller; shrink: *The camper's food supply began to dwindle after two weeks.*

ear·ly (ûr′ lē) *adj.* **ear·li·er, ear·li·est.** In the first part; near the beginning of a time period: *the early morning.*

earn (ûrn) *v.* **earned, earn·ing. 1.** To get money in return for working: *to earn a living.* **2.** To win by one's efforts: *The actor earned an award.*

earth (ûrth) *n.* Often **Earth. 1.** The third planet in the solar system. It is the planet on which human beings live. **2.** Soil; dirt.

eas·y (ē′ zē) *adj.* **eas·i·er, eas·i·est.** Not difficult: *an easy test.*

ech·o (ĕk′ ō) *n., pl.* **ech·oes.** A series of reflected sound waves; repeated sound.

edge (ĕj) *n.* **1.** The place or point where something begins or ends: *the edge of the woods.* **2.** The rim or brink of something: *the edge of the cliff.*

eight (āt) *n.* A number that is one more than seven. *These sound alike:* **eight, ate.**

el·bow (ĕl′ bō) *n.* The joint between the forearm and upper arm.

em·ploy (ĕm ploi′) *v.* **em·ployed, em·ploy·ing.** To hire and provide a livelihood for: *Mr. Jones employs four mechanics.*

em·ploy·er (ĕm ploi′ ər) *n.* A person or business that employs one or more persons.

en·clo·sure (ĕn klō′ zhər) *n.* Something that surrounds on all sides: *Our fence is an enclosure for our yard.*

en·coun·ter (ĕn koun′ tər) *v.* **en·coun·tered, en·coun·ter·ing.** To meet, especially unexpectedly or briefly: *It was funny to encounter my teacher on a Saturday.*

en·er·gy (ĕn′ ər jē) *n., pl.* **en·er·gies.** The ability or capability to put forth effort: *It takes energy to mow a yard.*

en·joy (ĕn joi′) *v.* **en·joyed, en·joy·ing.** To take pleasure in: *I enjoyed that play!*

e·nough (ĭ nŭf′) *adj.* Sufficient to satisfy a need: *enough money for the movie.*

e·rupt (ĭ rŭpt′) *v.* **e·rupt·ed, e·rupt·ing. 1.** To burst out suddenly; explode: *She was quiet, but I felt she might suddenly erupt into anger.* **2.** To become active and release lava: *No one knows when the volcano will erupt.*

eve·ning (ēv′ nĭng) *n.* The period of time just after sunset.

ev·er (ĕv′ ər) *adv.* **1.** At all times; always: *He is ever ready to help.* **2.** At any time: *Did you ever hear her sing?*

eve·ry (ĕv′ rē) *adj.* Each one of the entire number: *Every seat was filled.*

eve·ry·bod·y (ĕv′ rē bŏd′ ē) *or* (-bŭd′-) *pron.* Every person; everyone.

eve·ry·where (ĕv′ rē wâr′) *adv.* In all places.

ex·ot·ic (ĭg zŏt′ ĭk) *adj.* Foreign; unusual; strange: *The zoo has many exotic birds.*

ex·plode (ĭk splōd′) *v.* **ex·plod·ed, ex·plod·ing. 1.** To release energy with a loud noise: *The dynamite exploded.* **2.** To burst forth noisily: *The class exploded into laughter.*

ex·plore (ĭk splôr′) *v.* **ex·plored, ex·plor·ing.** To travel through an unknown place for the purpose of discovery: *explore the ocean.*

eye·sight (ī′ sīt′) *n.* The ability to see; vision: *Hawks have good eyesight.*

F Abbreviation of **Fahrenheit.**

fair (fâr) *adj.* **fair·er, fair·est. 1.** Just; not favoring one more than another: *a fair judge.* **2.** According to the rules: *a fair game.* **3.** Clear: *fair weather.* —*n.* A market. *These sound alike:* **fair, fare.**

fam·i·ly (făm′ ə lē) *or* (făm′ lē) *n., pl.* **fam·i·lies. 1.** A parent or parents and children. **2.** All of a person's relatives.

fare (fâr) *n.* The money one pays for the cost of traveling by train, plane, bus, etc. *These sound alike:* **fare, fair.**

farm·land (färm′ lănd′) *n.* Land that is used for farming: *Corn was planted on the farmland.*

fa·tigue (fə tēg′) *n.* The condition of being very tired or exhausted: *Mario went to bed early because of his fatigue.*

Feb·ru·ar·y (fĕb′ rōō ĕr′ ē) *or* (-yōō-) *n.* The second month of the year. It usually has 28 days but in leap year has 29.

feet Look up **foot.**

fence (fĕns) *n.* A railing, wall, or barrier made of boards, posts, etc. —*v.* **fenced, fenc·ing.** To enclose with a fence: *We fenced our backyard.*

fes·tiv·i·ty (fĕ stĭv′ ĭ tē) *n., pl.* **fes·tiv·i·ties.** An activity or event that is part of observing a special occasion: *The festivities included a fireworks show.*

fight (fīt) *v.* **fought, fight·ing. 1.** To struggle or combat with hands or weapons: *The army fought off the enemy.* **2.** To struggle in any way: *to fight for equality.* **3.** To try to overcome: *fight against cancer.*

flight (flīt) *n.* **1.** The act of flying: *a bird in flight.* **2.** An airline trip.

foe (fō) *n.* An enemy: *Is he a friend or foe?*

foot (fŏŏt) *n., pl.* **feet** (fēt). **1.** The part of the leg that touches the ground. **2.** Any base that resembles a foot: *foot of a chair.* **3.** A unit of length equal to 12 inches.

for·ev·er (fər ĕv′ ər) *adv.* Always; for all time.

for·get (fər gĕt′) *or* (fôr-) *v.* **for·got** (fər gŏt′) *or* (fôr-), **for·got·ten, for·got, for·get·ting.** To fail to remember.

for·got Look up **forget.**

for·ti·fy (fôr′ tə fī′) *v.* **for·ti·fied, for·ti·fy·ing, for·ti·fies.** To make stronger or more secure: *The steel rods fortified the walls.*

fox (fŏks) *n., pl.* **fox·es. 1.** A wild animal with a bushy tail and a pointed muzzle: *The fox turned and ran into the woods.* **2.** A clever person.

freeze (frēz) *v.* **froze** (frōz), **fro·zen, freez·ing. 1.** To turn from liquid to solid by removal of heat. **2.** To become covered with or turn to ice: *The pond froze.* **3.** To become motionless: *freeze with fear.*

Fri·day (frī′ dē) *or* (-dā′) *n.* The sixth day of the week.

friend (frĕnd) *n.* A person who knows and likes another.

front (frŭnt) *n.* The forward or first part of a thing or place: *The chalkboard is at the front of the room.*

froze Look up **freeze.**

fruit (frōōt) *n., pl.* **fruit** or **fruits.** The juicy, fleshy, seed-bearing part of a flowering plant.

ft Abbreviation of **foot.**

fudge (fŭj) *n.* A soft candy usually made with chocolate.

full (fŏŏl) *adj.* **full·er, full·est.**
1. Containing all that is possible; leaving no empty space: *a full tank.* **2.** Having a great many: *a room full of people.*

g Abbreviation of **gram.**

gal Abbreviation of **gallon.**

gal·ax·y (găl′ ək sē) *n., pl.* **gal·ax·ies.** A group of billions of stars.

geese Look up **goose.**

germ (jûrm) *n.* A tiny organism that causes disease.

gi·ant (jī′ ənt) *n.* Something (or someone) of great size or importance: *a sports giant.* —*adj.* Huge: *a giant watermelon.*

glad (glăd) *adj.* **glad·der, glad·dest.**
1. Feeling pleasure or joy: *I'm glad you're here.* **2.** Willing: *glad to help.*

glove (glŭv) *n., pl.* **gloves.** A covering for the hand with separate sections for the fingers and the thumb.

go (gō) *v.* **went, gone** (gôn) *or* (gŏn), **go·ing, goes** (gōz). **1.** To move along: *We're going to the store.* **2.** To depart: *You'd better go before you miss the bus.*

goes Look up **go.**

gone (gôn) *or* (gŏn) *adj.* **1.** Passed: *Summer is gone now.* **2.** Absent: *My parents will be gone for two weeks.*

good-bye or **goodbye** also **good-by** (gŏŏd′ bī′) *interj.* An expression used to acknowledge parting; farewell.

goose (gōōs) *n., pl.* **geese** (gēs). A water bird like a duck but larger and having a longer neck.

Gov. Abbreviation of **Governor.**

grass (grăs) *n.* Green bladed plants that cover lawns, fields, and pastures.

grav·i·ty (grăv′ ĭ tē) *n.* The force that causes objects to move toward the center of the earth.

grew Look up **grow.**

group (grōōp) *n.* **1.** A number of persons or things gathered together. **2.** People or things classed together because of similar qualities: *the vegetable group.*

grow (grō) *v.* **grew** (grōō), **grown, grow·ing.** To become large in size: *Most plants won't grow unless they have water.*

growl (groul) *n.* A low, deep, angry sound: *the dog's growl.* —*v.* **growled, growl·ing.** To make such a sound: *The dog growled at the mailman.*

guess (gĕs) *v.* **1.** To give an answer without really knowing. **2.** To think or believe: *I guess that's true!*

gui·tar (gĭ tär′) *n.* A musical instrument with strings, a fretted neck, and a pear-shaped sound box.

gym (jĭm) *n. Informal.* A gymnasium.

gym·na·si·um (jĭm **nā′** zē əm) *n.* A large room used for indoor sports.

Gyp·sy (jĭp′ sē) *n., pl.* **Gyp·sies.** A person who belongs to a wandering group of people who came to Europe from India long ago and now live all over the world.

had·n't (hăd′ nt) Contraction of **had not.**

half (hăf) *n., pl.* **halves** (hăvz) or (hävz). One of two equal parts into which something is divided.

hap·pen (hăp′ ən) *v.* **hap·pened, hap·pen·ing. 1.** To come to pass: *How did this happen?* **2.** To have the fortune: *I happened to see Jake on the bus.*

have·n't (hăv′ ənt) Contraction of **have not.**

health (hĕlth) *n.* **1.** The condition of the body. **2.** A freedom from sickness or disease.

hear (hîr) *v.* **heard** (hûrd), **hear·ing. 1.** To take in sounds through one's ears: *Did you hear the siren?* **2.** To listen: *He loved to hear stories of the West!* **3.** To receive news: *I heard that my principal retired. These sound alike:* **hear, here.**

heard Look up **hear.**

heart (härt) *n.* **1.** The hollow muscular organ that pumps blood to the arteries and receives blood from the veins. **2.** The center of someone's feelings and spirit.

heav·y (hĕv′ ē) *adj.* **heav·i·er, heav·i·est. 1.** Having great weight. **2.** Having a large amount: *a heavy snow.*

here (hîr) *adv.* In this place: *My dad's vegetable garden is here. These sound alike:* **here, hear.**

high (hī) *adj.* **high·er, high·est. 1.** Extending far up; tall: *twenty feet high.* **2.** Far above the ground: *a high branch.* **3.** Above average: *high grades.*

high·way (hī′ wā′) *n.* A main public road that usually connects cities and towns.

hike (hīk) *v.* **hiked, hik·ing.** To take a long walk, especially for pleasure. *—n., pl.* **hikes.** A long walk or trip on foot.

hoard (hôrd) *v.* **hoard·ed, hoard·ing.** To set aside and hide away: *Akio likes to hoard his gum instead of chewing it.*

hob·by (hŏb′ ē) *n., pl.* **hob·bies.** A favorite pastime or activity that one likes to do: *My hobby is collecting dollhouse furniture.*

hol·low (hŏl′ ō) *adj.* **hol·low·er, hol·low·est.** Having an opening inside; not solid; empty: *a hollow tree.*

hope (hōp) *v.* **hoped, hop·ing.** To look forward to something with confidence that it will happen: *She hopes to become a teacher.* *—n.* A feeling of confidence: *Her words gave us hope.*

hos·pi·tal (hŏs′ pĭ tl) or (-pĭt′ l) *n.* A place that provides medical and surgical care for the sick or injured.

host (hōst) *n.* A person who entertains guests: *The host of the party welcomed the guests.*

ho·tel (hō tĕl′) *n.* A house or large building that offers lodging and food to paying travelers, customers, etc.

hour (our) *n., pl.* **hours. 1.** A unit of time equal to 1/12 of the time between midnight and noon; 60 minutes. **2.** A particular time of day: *the lunch hour.*

hov·er (hŭv′ ər) or (hŏv′-) *v.* **hov·ered, hov·er·ing.** To stay in one place, floating, flying, or fluttering in the air: *The helicopter hovered over the landing pad.*

hun·dred (hŭn′ drĭd) *n.* A number that is equal to 10 times 10, written as 100.

hun·gry (hŭng′ grē) *adj.* **hun·gri·er, hun·gri·est. 1.** Desiring or needing food. **2.** Showing hunger: *The child had a hungry look.*

hunt (hŭnt) *v.* **hunt·ed, hunt·ing. 1.** To seek out to capture or kill for food or sport: *He hunts deer.* **2.** To search for: *Mom hunted for her keys. —n.* A hunting trip: *a fox hunt.*

hus·tle (hŭs′ əl) *v.* **hus·tled, hus·tling.** To hurry, move, or do quickly: *Maria hustled to her classroom.*

Hwy. Abbreviation of **highway.**

I'm (īm) Contraction of **I am.**

im·port (ĭm pôrt') *or* (ĭm' pôrt) *v.*
im·port·ed, im·port·ing. To bring in
products or goods from another country for
use or sale: *The grocery store is importing fruit
during the winter.*

im·por·tant (ĭm pôr' tnt) *adj.* **1.** Having a
great value: *an important speech.* **2.** Famous:
The President is an important person.

in Abbreviation of **inch.**

inch (ĭnch) *n., pl.* **inch·es.** A unit of length
equal to 1/12 of a foot.

in·side (ĭn' sīd') *or* (ĭn sīd') *adv.* Into or in
the inner part; within: *ran inside.*

in·ter·est·ing (ĭn' trĭ stĭng) *or* (-tər ĭ stĭng)
or (-tə rĕs' tĭng) *adj.* Able to capture and
hold one's attention: *an interesting TV
program.*

in·te·ri·or (ĭn tîr' ē ər) *n.* The inner side
or part; inside: *interior of the building.*

in·vite (ĭn vīt') *v.* **in·vit·ed, in·vit·ing.**
To ask someone to come somewhere or do
something: *Shaun will invite several guests
for dinner.*

i·ron (ī' ərn) *n.* **1.** A hard, gray metal.
2. A metal tool used to press clothes.
3. Great strength: *a will of iron.*
—*v.* **i·roned, i·ron·ing.** To press: *iron
a shirt.*

is·n't (ĭz' ənt) Contraction of **is not.**

itch (ĭch) *n.* A tickling feeling in the skin that
makes one want to scratch. —*v.* **itched,
itch·ing.** To have, feel, or cause an itch:
My elbow itches.

it'd (ĭt' əd) **1.** Contraction of **it would.**
2. Contraction of **it had.**

Jan·u·ar·y (jăn' yoō ĕr' ē) *n.* The first
month of the year.

jog (jŏg) *v.* **jogged, jog·ging. 1.** To shake
up: *jog my memory.* **2.** To run: *Paul jogged
around the track.*

Pronunciation Key

ă	pat	ŏ	pot	ŭ	cut
ā	pay	ō	toe	ûr	urge
âr	care	ô	paw, for	ə	about,
ä	father	oi	noise		item,
ĕ	pet	oŏ	took		edible,
ē	bee	oō	boot		gallop,
ĭ	pit	ou	out		circus
ī	pie	th	thin	ər	butter
îr	deer	*th*	this		

join (join) *v.* **joined, join·ing. 1.** To
connect or link: *join hands to form a circle.*
2. To become a part of: *join a club.*

Jr. Abbreviation of **junior.**

Ju·ly (joō lī') *n.* The seventh month of
the year.

June (joōn) *n.* The sixth month of the year.

jun·gle (jŭng' gəl) *n.*
A thick growth of
tropical bushes, vines,
trees, etc., extending
over a large area.

Ju·pi·ter (joō' pĭ tər) *n.*
The fifth planet of the
solar system in order of
distance from the sun.

ken·nel (kĕn' əl) *n.* **1.** A shelter where dogs
are kept. **2.** A place where dogs are raised,
trained, or cared for while their owners
are away.

kg Abbreviation of **kilogram.**

km Abbreviation of **kilometer.**

knee (nē) *n.* The joint between the thigh and
the lower leg.

knew Look up **know.** *These sound alike:*
knew, new.

knife (nīf) *n., pl.* **knives** (nīvz). A cutting
instrument with a sharp blade and a handle.

knock (nŏk) *v.* **knocked, knock·ing. 1.** To
hit or strike with the fist: *knock on the head.*
2. To make a noise by hitting on the surface:
knock on the door.

knot (nŏt) *n.* A fastening made by tying cord, rope, thread, etc. —*v.* **knot·ted, knot·ting.** To tie together: *She knotted the thread.*

know (nō) *v.* **knew** (no͞o) *or* (nyo͞o) **known, know·ing, knows** (nōz). **1.** To have the facts about: *She knows her spelling words.* **2.** To be skilled in: *He knows how to type.* **3.** To recognize: *I know that song!*

knuck·le (nŭk′ əl) *n.* A joint of a finger, especially one between a finger and the rest of the hand.

l Abbreviation of **liter.**

large (lärj) *adj.* **larg·er, larg·est.** Greater than average in size, number, etc; big.

lar·va (lär′ və) *n., pl.* **lar·vae** (lär′ vē) *or* **larvas.** The newly hatched, wormlike form of some insects.

laugh (lăf) *v.* **laughed, laugh·ing.** To make sounds and movements to show happiness: *The audience laughed at the clown.*

lawn (lôn) *n.* A piece of ground covered with close-cut grass, usually near a house.

lb Abbreviation of **pound.**

leaf (lēf) *n., pl.* **leaves** (lēvz). A thin, flat, green part of a tree or plant that grows on the stem.

learn (lûrn) *v.* **learned** *also* **learnt** (lûrnt), **learn·ing. 1.** To gain knowledge or skill: *to learn the multiplication tables.* **2.** To find out: *We learned that the game was cancelled.*

let's (lĕts) Contraction of **let us.**

life (līf) *n., pl.* **lives** (līvz). **1.** The property of living organisms that includes the ability to grow and reproduce. **2.** The period of time between birth and death. **3.** Living organisms: *plant life.*

light·ning (līt′ nĭng) *n.* An electrical discharge in the atmosphere.

light·weight (līt′ wāt′) *adj.* Not weighing much; not heavy: *lightweight clothing.*

loose (lo͞os) *adj.* **loos·er, loos·est. 1.** Not fastened tightly or securely: *a loose button.* **2.** Not shut in; free: *The dog was loose in our backyard.*

loud (loud) *adj.* **loud·er, loud·est.** Making or having a strong sound: *a loud voice.*

love·ly (lŭv′ lē) *adj.* **love·li·er, love·li·est.** Having pleasing qualities; beautiful: *Those are the loveliest flowers in our garden.*

loy·al (loi′ əl) *adj.* True and faithful to a person, country, etc.

loy·al·ty (loi′ əl tē) *n.* The condition of being faithful.

m Abbreviation of **meter.**

mag·ic (măj′ ĭk) *n.* **1.** The art or pretended art of controlling forces through the use of secret charms. **2.** Special effects and tricks using quickness of hands. —*adj.* Having to do with magic: *a magic show.*

man (măn) *n., pl.* **men** (mĕn). An adult male person.

mar·ble (mär′ bəl) *n., pl.* **mar·bles. 1.** Small, colored glass balls used in games. **2. marbles.** Children's game played with such balls.

March (märch) *n.* The third month of the year.

Mars (märz) *n.* The fourth planet of the solar system in order of distance from the sun.

match¹ (măch) *n.* **1.** Person or thing equal to another: *his match at tennis.* **2.** A sports contest: *a tennis match.* —*v.* **matched, match·ing. 1.** To be alike: *These shoes match.* **2.** To correspond to: *He matched her running pace.*

match² (măch) *n.* A strip of cardboard or wood with a substance that catches fire when rubbed on a rough surface.

may (mā) *aux. v.* **might** (mīt). **1.** Used to indicate possibility: *It may snow.* **2.** To be allowed or permitted to: *May I have a cookie?*

May (mā) *n.* The fifth month of the year.

mean (mēn) *v.* **meant, mean·ing, means** (mēnz). **1.** To have the sense of: *This means war.* **2.** To intend: *She meant to be helpful.*

meek (mēk) *adj.* **meek•er, meek•est.**
1. Patient; gentle. 2. Not fighting back.

men Look up **man.**

Mer•cu•ry (mûr′ kyə rē) *n.* The planet of the solar system that is closest to the sun.

me•te•or (mē′ tē ər) *or* (-ôr′) *n.* A fragment of solid matter that enters the earth's atmosphere and burns, leaving a bright streak in the sky.

mi Abbreviation of **mile.**

mice Look up **mouse.**

mid•dle (mĭd′ l) *n.* 1. The point that is the same distance from each end; the center. 2. A point in time halfway between the beginning and the end: *middle of the day.*

mid•night (mĭd′ nīt′) *n.* Twelve o'clock at night. —*adj.* Of or at midnight: *a midnight ride.*

might¹ (mīt) *n.* Great power or strength: *the army's might.*

might² Look up **may.**

might•y (mī′ tē) *adj.* **might•i•er, might•i•est.** Having great power or strength; strong.

mis•sile (mĭs′ əl) *or* (mĭs′ īl′) *n.* An object, such as an arrow, bullet, or other weapon that is shot through the air at a target.

mis•take (mĭ stāk′) *n.* An act or choice that is wrong. —*v.* **mis•took, mis•tak•en, mis•tak•ing.** To misunderstand what one sees or hears: *I mistook that raccoon for a cat.*

mis•un•der•stand (mĭs′ ŭn dər stănd′) *v.* **mis•un•der•stood** (mĭs′ ŭn dər stŏod′), **mis•un•der•stand•ing.** To not understand.

mis•un•der•stood Look up **misunderstand.**

mod•el (mŏd′ l) *n.* 1. A small copy of something. 2. A person or thing that is a good example: *To write our report, we studied the model.* 3. Someone who wears clothes for advertisement. —*v.* **mod•eled, mod•el•ing.** 1. To copy. 2. To display by wearing.

mois•ture (mois′ chər) *n.* Wetness caused by water.

Mon•day (mŭn′ dē) *or* (-dā) *n.* The second day of the week, following Sunday and coming before Tuesday.

mon•ey (mŭn′ ē) *n., pl.* **mon•eys** or **mon•ies.** Coins or paper notes of fixed value made to use in exchange for goods or services.

mon•goose (mŏng′ gōos′) *or* (mŏn′ gōos′) *n.* A slender animal with a pointed face, a long tail, and the ability to catch and kill poisonous snakes.

mon•key (mŭng′ kē) *n., pl.* **mon•keys.** An animal having hands with thumbs, particularly the smaller, long-tailed animals.

month (mŭnth) *n.* One of the 12 parts into which a year is divided.

morn•ing (môr′ nĭng) *n.* The early part of the day, ending with noon.

mo•tor (mō′ tər) *n.* An engine; something that produces mechanical power. —*adj.* Propelled by a motor: *a motor scooter.*

mouse (mous) *n., pl.* **mice** (mīs). A small animal with a long, narrow tail.

mouth (mouth) *n., pl.* **mouths** (mou*th*z). 1. The opening through which animals take in food. 2. A natural opening: *the mouth of the cave.* 3. The opening of a container: *the mouth of a jar.*

Ms. or **Ms** (mĭs) *or* (mĭz) Abbreviation used as a title before a woman's last name whether or not she is married.

must•'ve (mŭst′ əv) Contraction of **must have.**

neigh·bor (nā′ bər) *n.* Someone who lives next door or nearby.

Nep·tune (nĕp′ tōōn′) *or* (-tyōōn′) *n.* The eighth planet of the solar system in order of distance from the sun.

nev·er (nĕv′ ər) *adv.* At no time; not ever: *I have never seen the Grand Canyon.*

new (nōō) *or* (nyōō) *adj.* **new·er, new·est.** **1.** Recently made or formed: *a new bridge.* **2.** Just learned or discovered: *a new theory.* **3.** Never used: *a new pair of shoes.* **4.** Unfamiliar: *new surroundings. These sound alike:* **new, knew.**

news·pa·per (nōōz′ pā′ pər) *or* (nyōōz′-) *n.* A daily or weekly publication printed on large sheets of paper folded together, telling current news and carrying advertisements, announcements, etc.

night (nīt) *n.* **1.** The time between sunset and sunrise when it is dark. **2.** An evening devoted to a special event: *The actor was nervous on opening night. These sound alike:* **night, knight.**

night·mare (nīt′ mâr′) *n.* **1.** A frightening dream. **2.** A frightening experience: *The volcano was a nightmare!*

noise (noiz) *n.* **1.** A loud, harsh sound: *The noise of traffic kept me awake.* **2.** Sound of any kind: *the noise of boat whistles.*

north (nôrth) *n.* **1.** The direction 90° counterclockwise from the east, just opposite south. **2.** A region of the earth in this direction. —*adv.* Of or in the north.

nose (nōz) *n.* **1.** The part of the face that contains the nostrils and organs of smell. **2.** The sense of smell: *Mike's nose told him dinner was fried fish!* **3.** The front part of a plane, rocket, etc.

note·book (nōt′ bŏŏk′) *n.* A book in which to write notes to be remembered or learned: *my science notebook.*

noth·ing (nŭth′ ĭng) *pron.* Not anything: *Ella had nothing to do.*

noun (noun) *n.* A word used as the name of a person, place, thing, event, or quality.

No·vem·ber (nō vĕm′ bər) *n.* The eleventh month of the year.

oak (ōk) *n.* **1.** Any of several trees with irregularly notched leaves and acorns. **2.** The hard, durable wood of this tree: *The floor is made of oak.*

o·bey (ō bā′) *v.* **o·beyed, o·bey·ing.** **1.** To follow or carry out a request, order, or law: *obey the rules.* **2.** To do what is told: *obey the teacher.*

ob·ject[1] (ŏb′ jĕkt′) *n.* **1.** Something that can be seen or touched: *a round object, a metal object.* **2.** A goal or purpose: *the object of the quiz.*

ob·ject[2] (əb jĕkt′) *v.* **ob·ject·ed, ob·ject·ing.** To oppose or protest: *The guards will object to longer working hours.*

o·cean (ō′ shən) *n.* **1.** The large mass of salt water that covers almost three fourths of the earth's surface. **2.** Any of the main divisions of this water, such as the Atlantic Ocean.

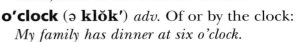

o'clock (ə klŏk′) *adv.* Of or by the clock: *My family has dinner at six o'clock.*

Oc·to·ber (ŏk tō′ bər) *n.* The tenth month of the year.

of·fer (ô′ fər) *or* (ŏf′ ər) *v.* **of·fered, of·fer·ing.** To present to be accepted or refused: *She offered us some candy.*

of·fer·ing (ô′ fər ĭng) *or* (ŏf′ ər ĭng) *n., pl.* **of·fer·ings.** A gift or contribution.

of·fice (ô′ fĭs) *or* (ŏf′ ĭs) *n.* **1.** A place in which business or professional work is done: *the lawyer's office.* **2.** A position: *The class held elections for the office of president.*

of·ten (ô′ fən) *or* (ŏf′ ən) *adv.* Many times; frequently.

once (wŭns) *adv.* **1.** One time: *Take your vitamins once each day.* **2.** At one time in the past: *the once-great ruler.*

on·ly (ōn′ lē) *adj.* One and no more; sole: *an only child.* —*adv.* Merely; just: *Only two bananas are left.*

or·bit (ôr′ bĭt) *n.* The path of a planet, satellite, or heavenly body around another body in space: *the earth's orbit around the sun.* —*v.* **or·bit·ed, or·bit·ing.** To put into or move about in an orbit: *The spacecraft orbits the earth.*

oth·er (ŭ*th*′ ər) *adj.* **1.** Being the remaining one: *The other cake looks fresher.* **2.** Different: *Let's play some other game.* **3.** Extra; additional: *I have no other belt that matches this dress.* —*n.* The remaining one: *One twin likes golf; the other likes tennis.*

ours (ourz) *pron.* A possessive form of **we.** The one or ones that belong to us: *They lost their ball, but we have ours.*

out·side (out sīd′) *or* (out′ sīd′) *n.* The outer part or surface: *the outside of the box.* —*adv.* On or to the outside: *I'm going outside with Scotty!*

o·ver·lap (ō′ vər lăp′) *v.* **o·ver·lapped, o·ver·lap·ping.** To rest on top of or over something and cover a part of it: *This fish scale is overlapping the one beneath.*

own (ōn) *adj.* Of or belonging to oneself or itself: *my own car.* —*v.* **owned, own·ing.** To have or possess: *My parents own the house they are living in.*

ox (ŏks) *n., pl.* **ox·en** (ŏk′ sən). A full-grown male of domestic cattle that are used for farm work.

ox·en Look up **ox.**

oz Abbreviation of **ounce.**

pack·age (păk′ ĭj) *n.* A box or bundle containing one or more objects: *We received a package in the mail.* —*v.* **pack·aged, pack·ag·ing.** To place in a package.

paid Look up **pay.**

Pronunciation Key

ă	pat	ŏ	pot	ŭ	cut
ā	pay	ō	toe	ûr	urge
âr	care	ô	paw, for	ə	about,
ä	father	oi	noise		item,
ě	pet	ŏŏ	took		edible,
ē	bee	ōō	boot		gallop,
ĭ	pit	ou	out		circus
ī	pie	th	thin	ər	butter
îr	deer	*th*	this		

pass (păs) *v.* **passed, pass·ing. 1.** To go by: *We passed the carnival in the center of town.* **2.** To go through: *Oil passes through a pipe.* **3.** To be successful: *pass the math test.* **4.** To go by in time: *He passed the hours playing his guitar.*

past (păst) *adj.* Gone by; over: *The winter is past.* —*n.* Time gone by: *We learn from the past.* —*prep.* Beyond in time: *past midnight.*

pat·i·o (păt′ ē ō′) *n., pl.* **pat·i·os.** A paved outdoor space that is used for eating, cooking, or relaxing: *Tina's and Sara's patios are separated by a fence.*

pause (pôz) *n.* A break in action or speech: *There was a brief pause for a commercial.* —*v.* **paused, paus·ing.** To stop in action or speech: *The speaker paused to clear her throat.*

pay (pā) *v.* **paid** (pād), **pay·ing.** To give money for goods or services: *We pay the baby sitter $3.00 an hour.*

peace (pēs) *n.* **1.** Freedom from war. **2.** A calm, ordered condition: *peace and quiet.*

peach (pēch) *n., pl.* **peach·es. 1.** A sweet, round fruit with yellowish skin and a rough pit. **2.** A yellowish-pink color.

pen·ny (pĕn′ ē) *n., pl.* **pen·nies.** A United States or Canadian coin worth one hundredth of a dollar.

peo·ple (pē′ pəl) *n., pl.* **peo·ple. 1.** Human beings; men, women, and children: *The bus seats 80 people.* **2.** A nation: *the Norwegian people.*

pe·ri·od (pîr′ ē əd) *n.* **1.** A portion of time having a specific length or character: *a period of two months.* **2.** A punctuation mark used at the end of certain sentences.

phys·ics (fĭz′ ĭks) *n.* A science that deals with matter and energy and the laws governing them. Physics includes the study of light, motion, sound, heat, electricity, and force.

pi·an·o (pē ăn′ ō) *n., pl.* **pi·an·os.** A keyboard musical instrument in which the player sets off sound by striking the keys with the fingers.

pic·nic (pĭk′ nĭk) *n.* A pleasure trip with a meal eaten in the open air: *We went on a picnic.*

pic·ture (pĭk′ chər) *n.* **1.** A visual representation such as a drawing, painting, photograph, etc.

pil·low (pĭl′ ō) *n.* A cloth case stuffed with feathers, down, or other soft material used to support the head while sleeping.

pitch (pĭch) *v.* **pitched, pitch·ing. 1.** To throw: *pitch a horseshoe.* **2.** In baseball, to throw a ball from the mound to the batter.

piz·za (pēt′ sə) *n.* A shallow, pie-like crust covered with cheese, tomato sauce, and spices. Italian in origin.

plain (plān) *adj.* **plain·er, plain·est. 1.** Easy to understand: *plain talk.* **2.** Clear; open to view: *in plain sight.* **3.** Simple: *a plain dress. These sound alike:* **plain, plane.**

plane (plān) *n.* **1.** A flat or level surface. **2.** An airplane. *These sound alike:* **plane, plain.**

plan·et (plăn′ ĭt) *n. pl.* **plan·ets.** A heavenly body that moves around the sun in a fixed orbit.

plas·tic (plăs′ tĭk) *n.* Any of a group of substances made chemically and molded by heat to form sheets, fibers, bottles, etc.

please (plēz) *v.* **pleased, pleas·ing. 1.** To give pleasure to: *The gift pleased Mom.* **2.** To wish: *Frank does as he pleases.*

plen·ty (plĕn′ tē) *n.* A full supply; all that is needed: *plenty of food.*

Plu·to (plōō′ tō) *n.* The ninth planet of the solar system in order of distance from the sun.

pock·et (pŏk′ ĭt) *n., pl.* **pock·ets.** A small pouch sewn into clothing and used to hold things.

po·em (pō′ əm) *n.* A composition, usually in verse, with language meant to vividly express an image or experience.

point (point) *n.* **1.** The sharp end of something: *the point of the pencil.* **2.** A place or position: *the starting point.*

point·less (point′ lĭs) *adj.* Senseless; meaningless: *Juan thought the argument was pointless.*

poise (poiz) *n.* Calmness and confidence: *Poise will help you impress others.* —*v.* **poised, pois·ing.** To balance or be balanced: *The cat poised for the jump onto the table.*

poi·son (poi′ zən) *n.* Any substance dangerous to life and health: *Bottles containing poison are clearly marked.* —*v.* **poi·soned, poi·son·ing.** To kill or harm with poison.

po·lice (pə lēs′) *n., pl.* **po·lice. 1.** The part of the government that maintains order and enforces the law. **2.** The members of this department.

po·ny (pō′ nē) *n., pl.* **po·nies.** Any of several kinds of small horses.

pop·corn (pŏp′ kôrn′) *n.* A kind of corn with kernels that burst open and puff out when heated.

pow·er·ful (pou′ ər fəl) *adj.* Having great power or force: *a powerful engine; a powerful country.*

pre·cau·tion (prĭ kô′ shən) *n.* Something that is done beforehand to guard against harm, danger, mistakes, or accidents.

Pres. Abbreviation of **President.**

prob·lem (prŏb′ ləm) *n.* Something that needs to be solved or worked out: *a math problem; the problem of world hunger.*

pro·gram (prō′ grăm) *or* (-grəm) *n.* **1.** An ordered list of events for a performance, presentation, etc. **2.** The performance or presentation; a show.

proud (proud) *adj.* **proud·er, proud·est. 1.** Feeling of pleasure over something one owns, is, or does: *proud to be a farmer.* **2.** Having self-respect.

pt Abbreviation of **pint.**

pud·ding (po͝od′ ĭng) *n.* A sweet, custard-like dessert: *chocolate pudding.*

pull (po͝ol) *v.* **pulled, pull·ing. 1.** To move toward oneself through grasping and drawing with force: *pulling the cart.* **2.** To put on: *pull on the mittens.*

pur·ple (pûr′ pəl) *n.* A color produced by mixing red and blue pigments. —*adj.* Of that color: *a purple dress.*

qt Abbreviation of **quart.**

quart (kwôrt) *n.* A unit of volume used for measuring liquid, equal to two pints.

queen (kwēn) *n.* **1.** A female monarch: *Queen Elizabeth.* **2.** A woman who is very important: *the queen of jazz.*

quick (kwĭk) *adj.* **quick·er, quick·est. 1.** Moving with speed; fast: *The cowboy was quick on the draw.* **2.** Done in a short time: *a quick lunch.* **3.** Bright; alert: *a quick mind.*

qui·et (kwī′ ĭt) *adj.* **qui·et·er, qui·et·est. 1.** Making little or no sound: *the quiet baby.* **2.** Not moving; still: *The steamboat floated down the quiet river.*

qui·et·ness (kwī′ ĭt nəs) *or* (-nĭs′) *n.* Silence: *The quietness in the classroom was unusual.*

ra·di·o (rā′ dē ō) *n., pl.* **ra·di·os. 1.** The use of electromagnetic waves to carry messages without the use of wires. **2.** The equipment used to carry such sound. —*v.* **ra·di·oed, ra·di·o·ing.** To send messages in this manner.

rail·road (rāl′ rōd′) *n.* A road or track built with parallel steel rails and used by trains.

Rd. Abbreviation of **Road.**

read·y (rĕd′ ē) *adj.* **read·i·er, read·i·est. 1.** Prepared for action or use: *getting ready for the trip.* **2.** Willing: *ready to accept the offer.*

rea·son (rē′ zən) *n.* A cause for acting, thinking, or feeling a special way. —*v.* **rea·soned, rea·son·ing.** To conclude.

re·gard·less (rĭ gärd′ lĭs) *adv.* Without concern for problems or objections; anyway: *The children play outside regardless of the weather.*

reign (rān) *n.* The time that a king or queen rules. —*v.* **reigned, reign·ing.** To rule as a king or queen. *These sound alike:* **reign, rain, rein.**

re·ply (rĭ plī′) *v.* **re·plied, re·ply·ing.** To give an answer: *He replied with anger.* —*n.* An answer: *His reply was incorrect.*

re·port (rĭ pôrt′) *n.* An oral or written account containing information in an organized form: *Her report was about Brazil.* —*v.* **re·port·ed, re·port·ing.** To give an account of something: *report the baseball scores.*

re·trieve (rĭ trēv′) *v.* **re·trieved, re·triev·ing.** To get back: *We will retrieve the baseballs we hit.*

re·vive (rĭ vīv′) *v.* **re·vived, re·viv·ing. 1.** To come or bring back to life or consciousness. **2.** To give new strength to.

re·volve (rĭ vŏlv′) *v.* **re·volved, re·volv·ing.** To move in a circle or orbit: *Planets revolve around the sun.*

right (rīt) *n.* **1.** The side opposite the left. **2.** That which is fitting or good: *right or wrong.* —*adj.* Of or located to the opposite of the left: *the right foot.*

rock¹ (rŏk) *n., pl.* **rocks. 1.** Any hard, natural material of mineral origin; stone. **2.** The mineral matter that makes up a large portion of the earth's crust.

rock² (rŏk) *v.* **rocked, rock·ing.** To move backward and forward, or from side to side: *The waves rocked the boat.*

ro·tate (rō′ tāt′) *v.* **ro·tat·ed, ro·tat·ing.** To turn around a center or axis.

rough (rŭf) *adj.* **rough·er, rough·est.**
1. Not smooth or even: *a rough trail.*
2. Coarse to the touch: *rough sandpaper.*
3. Not gentle: *a rough, tough bully.*

route (ro͞ot) *or* (rout) *n.* A road for traveling from one place to another: *We took the coastal route to Los Angeles. These sound alike:* **route, root.**

roy·al (roi′ əl) *adj.* **1.** Of kings and queens: *the royal palace.* **2.** Fit for a king or queen: *royal treatment.*

Rte. Abbreviation of **Route.**

ru·ral (ro͝or′ əl) *adj.* Having to do with, in, or like the country, country people, or life in the country: *My family bought a house in a rural area.*

sat·el·lite (săt′ l īt′) *n.*
1. A heavenly body that revolves around a planet: *The moon is a satellite of the earth.* **2.** An artificial object launched to orbit the earth or other celestial bodies.

Sat·ur·day (săt′ ər dē) *or* (-dā′) *n.* The seventh day of the week.

Sat·urn (săt′ ərn) *n.* The sixth planet of the solar system in order of distance from the sun.

save (sāv) *v.* **saved, sav·ing. 1.** To rescue from harm or danger. **2.** To keep for future use; to store: *Please save me some leftovers from dinner.*

scarf (skärf) *n., pl.* **scarfs** or **scarves** (skärvz). A triangular or rectangular piece of cloth worn around the head, neck, or shoulders: *Kristy's scarf was very colorful.*

score (skôr) *or* (skōr) *n.* The total number of points made by a player or team in a game or contest. —*v.* **scored, scor·ing.** To make points in a game or contest: *He scored 12 points.*

scream (skrēm) *v.* **screamed, scream·ing.** To make a loud, sharp cry. —*n.* A loud cry.

sea·son (sē′ zən) *n.* **1.** One of four divisions of the year: spring, summer, autumn, and winter. **2.** A time of the year devoted to a certain activity: *baseball season.*

se·cret (sē′ krĭt) *adj.* Kept from general knowledge: *secret missions.* —*n.* Something known only to oneself or a few: *Can you keep a secret?*

seem (sēm) *v.* **seemed, seem·ing.** To appear to be: *He seems angry about the judge's decision.*

Sep·tem·ber (sĕp tĕm′ bər) *n.* The ninth month of the year.

shad·ow (shăd′ ō) *n.* The outline cast by an object blocking the light's rays.

shall (shăl) *aux. v.* **should** (sho͝od). **1.** Used to express intention; will: *I shall go home tomorrow.* **2.** Used to express an order, rule, or duty; must: *You should wash your hands before you eat.*

shape (shāp) *n.* **1.** An outline or form: *the shape of a circle.* **2.** A form or condition in which something exists: *The old barn was in good shape.* —*v.* **shaped, shap·ing.** To mold or give a form to: *shape the clay.*

share (shâr) *v.* **shared, shar·ing. 1.** To use, experience, or enjoy with others: *share the pie.* **2.** To disclose to others: *share the information with the police.* —*n.* A portion: *a share of the estate.*

sharp (shärp) *adj.* **sharp·er, sharp·est.**
1. Having a thin cutting edge: *a sharp knife.*
2. Abrupt: *a sharp drop in the mountain.*
3. Clear: *a sharp picture.* **4.** Quick and forceful: *a sharp slap.* **5.** Having a strong odor or flavor: *a sharp taste.*

she'd (shēd) **1.** Contraction of **she had.** **2.** Contraction of **she would.**

sheep (shēp) *n., pl.* **sheep.** An animal with a fleecy coat that is used for wool.

shelf (shĕlf) *n., pl.* **shelves** (shĕlvz). A flat rectangular piece of metal, wood, etc. fastened to a wall and used to store things.

shelves Look up **shelf**.

sher•iff (shĕr′ ĭf) *n.* The county officer in charge of making sure the law is obeyed.

shoot (sho͞ot) *v.* **shot, shoot•ing. 1.** To hit, wound, or kill with a bullet, arrow, etc. **2.** To aim for: *shooting for a record-breaking marathon run.*

shore (shôr) *n.* The land along the edge of a sea, lake, etc.

should Look up **shall**.

should•n't (sho͝od′ nt) Contraction of **should not**.

should•'ve (sho͝od′ əv) Contraction of **should have**.

show•er (shou′ ər) *n.* **1.** A short fall of rain. **2.** A steady flow of something: *a shower of gifts.* **3.** A shower bath. **4.** A party to honor someone: *a baby shower.* —*v.* **show•ered, show•er•ing. 1.** To fall down as in a shower. **2.** To bestow: *The grandparents showered the baby with love.*

sight (sīt) *n.* **1.** The ability to see: *My sight is better with glasses.* **2.** Thing seen; something worth seeing: *the sight of Paris.*

sim•ple (sĭm′ pəl) *adj.* **sim•pler, sim•plest. 1.** Easy; not complicated: *a simple game.* **2.** Not showy: *a simple suit.*

size (sīz) *n.* **1.** The amount of space that something takes up: *These two boxes are the same size.* **2.** The extent or amount: *the size of the factory.*

ski (skē) *n., pl.* **skis.** One of a pair of long, flat, wood or metal runners used for gliding on snow or water. —*v.* **skied, ski•ing.** To glide or move on skis.

ski•er (skē′ ər) *n., pl.* **skiers.** A person who skis: *The beginning skier went down the low hill.*

skirt (skûrt) *n.* **1.** The part of a dress that hangs from the waist. **2.** A separate piece of clothing that hangs from the waist.

ă	pat	ŏ	pot	ŭ	cut
ā	pay	ō	toe	ûr	urge
âr	care	ô	paw, for	ə	about,
ä	father	oi	noise		item,
ĕ	pet	o͞o	took		edible,
ē	bee	ōō	boot		gallop,
ĭ	pit	ou	out		circus
ī	pie	th	thin	ər	butter
îr	deer	*th*	*th*is		

slide (slīd) *v.* **slid, slid•ing. 1.** To move smoothly along a surface: *to slide the drawers back and forth.* **2.** To slip: *slide on ice.* —*n.* A sliding action or movement: *a rock slide.*

slowly (slō′ lē) Not quickly.

smart (smärt) *adj.* **smart•er, smart•est. 1.** Bright; intelligent: *a smart child.* **2.** Fashionable: *a smart new dress.*

smile (smīl) *n.* An expression formed by the upward curve of the mouth to show pleasure, amusement, etc. —*v.* **smiled, smil•ing.** To look pleased or amused: *She smiled as she watched the playful dog.*

snack (snăk) *n.* **1.** A light meal. **2.** Food eaten between regular meals.

soap (sōp) *n.* A cleansing agent, usually made of fat and lye and manufactured as bars, flakes, or liquid.

soil¹ (soil) *n.* The top layer of the earth's surface in which seeds are planted; dirt.

soil² (soil) *v.* **soiled, soil•ing.** To make or become dirty: *Jarrell soiled his white T-shirt.*

solar system (sō′ lər sĭs′ təm) *n.* The sun and all the planets, satellites, etc., that revolve around it.

solve (sŏlv) *or* (sôlv) *v.* **solved, solv•ing.** To find the answer to: *She solved the problem by herself.*

some•how (sŭm′ hou′) *adv.* In some way: *I knew that I'd get there somehow.*

some•times (sŭm′ tīmz′) *adv.* At times or on several occasions: *It happens sometimes when I least expect it.*

sor·ry (sŏr′ ē) *adj.* **sor·ri·er, sor·ri·est.** Feeling pity or regret: *I'm sorry that you don't feel well.*

soup (sōōp) *n.* A liquid food made by boiling meat, vegetables, etc.

sour (sour) *adj.* **sour·er, sour·est. 1.** Having a sharp, biting taste; acid: *Lemonade is sour.* **2.** Spoiled: *sour milk.*

south (south) *n.* **1.** The direction 90° clockwise from the direction of the sunrise; just opposite north. **2.** The region of the earth that lies in this direction. —*adj.* Of or in the south.

sow (sō) *v.* **sowed, sown** or **sowed, sow·ing.** To scatter seeds over the ground to produce a crop: *Keesha will sow the carrot seeds in her garden. These sound alike:* **sow, sew, so.**

soy·bean (soi′ bēn′) *n.* Also **soya bean.** A bean plant grown for its edible, nutritious seeds.

space (spās) *n.* **1.** The unlimited area in which the solar system, stars, and galaxies exist. **2.** Any blank or empty area: *The space beside the tree will be used for my garden.*

speak (spēk) *v.* **spoke, spok·en, speak·ing. 1.** To utter words: *She spoke excitedly about horseback riding.* **2.** To give a speech: *The mayor will speak on TV.* **3.** To use a language: *I speak Spanish and French at my school.*

spe·cial (spĕsh′ əl) *adj.* **1.** Not common or usual; exceptional: *a special event.* **2.** Distinct from others: *a special lock that sets off an alarm.* **3.** Having a particular function or purpose: *special skills.*

speech (spēch) *n.* **1.** The act of speaking. **2.** The ability to speak. **3.** A talk or address: *the governor's speech.*

spoil (spoil) *v.* **spoiled** or **spoilt, spoil·ing. 1.** To damage or injure so as to make useless: *The bad weather spoiled the garden party.* **2.** To become rotten or decayed. **3.** To indulge too much: *spoil the child.*

sponge (spŭnj) *n.* **1.** A simple water animal having a soft, elastic skeleton with many pores. **2.** The absorbent skeleton of any of these animals, used for soaking, cleaning, etc.

spy (spī) *n., pl.* **spies. 1.** An agent paid to secretly obtain information. **2.** A person who secretly watches another. —*v.* **spied, spy·ing.** To keep secret watch: *The soldiers spied on the enemy.*

squad (skwŏd) *n.* **1.** A small group of soldiers who work, train, and fight together. **2.** A small group of people who work together toward a goal. **3.** A sports team.

square (skwâr) *n.* **1.** A rectangle with four equal sides. **2.** Any figure with this shape. **3.** An open area at the intersection of two streets.

squeeze (skwēz) *v.* **squeezed, squeez·ing. 1.** To press hard upon: *squeeze the stuffed animal.* **2.** To put pressure on to extract liquid: *squeeze a lemon.* **3.** To force one's way: *squeeze through the door.* **4.** To crowd: *squeeze into the bus.*

squirt (skwûrt) *v.* **squirt·ed, squirt·ing. 1.** To force out through a narrow opening. **2.** To come out in a jet or stream.

St. Abbreviation of **Street.**

stair (stâr) *n.*, often used in the plural **stairs.** A series or flight of steps. *These sound alike:* **stair, stare.**

stamp (stămp) *v.* **stamped, stamp·ing. 1.** To set the foot down heavily: *Stamp your wet shoes on the floor.* **2.** To strike with an object that leaves a mark or message. **3.** To put postage on. —*n.* **1.** An object that leaves a mark when pressed on something. **2.** A piece of gummed paper with a special mark: *a postage stamp.*

stand (stănd) *v.* **stood** (stōōd), **stand·ing.** To stay in an upright position on the feet.

stare (stâr) *v.* **stared, star·ing, stares.** To look at with a steady gaze: *Jasmine stared at the famous movie star. These sound alike:* **stare, stair.**

state (stāt) *n.* **1.** A condition: *the state of my bank account.* **2.** A mood: *an angry state.* **3.** A group of people living under an independent government: *the state of Israel.* **4.** One of 50 subdivisions of the United States: *the state of Virginia.*

steal (stēl) *v.* **stole** (stōl), **stol·en, steal·ing. 1.** To take without permission. **2.** To move or pass without making noise: *steal through the bushes.*

stole Look up **steal.**

stom·ach (stŭm′ ək) *n.* A large muscular bag in the body that receives food, digests some of it, and passes it on to the intestines.

stood Look up **stand.**

sto·ry (stôr′ ē) *or* (stōr′-) *n., pl.* **sto·ries.** An account of something either true or fictitious: *a story about a mountain adventure.*

stow (stō) *v.* **stowed, stow·ing.** To put away or store for future use; pack: *We stow our bicycles in the garage.*

straw (strô) *n.* Stalks of grain after drying and threshing used as stuffing or padding, or for weaving hats, baskets, etc.

stretch (strĕch) *v.* **stretched, stretch·ing. 1.** To draw out or pull: *Elastic stretches.* **2.** To extend across a given space: *This route stretches across two states.* **3.** To extend one's body or limbs: *stretch out on the couch.*

strong (strông) *or* (strŏng) *adj.* **strong·er, strong·est. 1.** Physically powerful: *a strong person.* **2.** Able to take stress or strain: *a strong chair.* **3.** Intense in degree: *strong feelings.*

stud·y (stŭd′ ē) *n., pl.* **stud·ies.** The effort to learn by reading and thinking: *hours of study.* —*v.* **stud·ied, stud·y·ing.** To apply one's mind to gaining knowledge: *to study science.*

sub·ject (sŭb′ jĭkt) *adj.* Under the power of another: *subject to the will of the king.* —*n.* **1.** A person or thing that something is about: *the subject of the book.* **2.** An area of study: *Music is my favorite subject.*

sud·den·ly (sŭd′ n lē) *adv.* Happening at once without warning: *The storm was suddenly upon us.*

Pronunciation Key

ă	pat	ŏ	pot	ŭ	cut
ā	pay	ō	toe	ûr	urge
âr	care	ô	paw, for	ə	about,
ä	father	oi	noise		item,
ĕ	pet	ŏŏ	took		edible,
ē	bee	ōō	boot		gallop,
ĭ	pit	ou	out		circus
ī	pie	th	thin	ər	butter
îr	deer	*th*	this		

sug·ar (shŏŏg′ ər) *n.* A sweet substance made from sugar cane or sugar beets and used in food products.

sum·mer (sŭm′ ər) *n.* The season of the year between spring and autumn.

Sun·day (sŭn′ dē) *or* (-dā′) *n.* The first day of the week.

sun·shine (sŭn′ shīn′) *n.* **1.** The light of the sun. **2.** Happiness.

sup·ply (sə plī′) *v.* **sup·plied, sup·ply·ing, sup·plies.** To provide: *Trees supply paper goods and wood products.* —*n.* The amount available: *Our pencil supply is low.*

sur·prise (sər prīz′) *v.* **sur·prised, sur·pris·ing.** To cause to feel astonished: *Our early arrival will surprise her.* —*n.* Something sudden and unexpected: *The party came as a surprise!*

swal·low¹ (swŏl′ ō) *v.* **swal·lowed, swal·low·ing.** To take into the stomach through the throat: *swallow food.*

swal·low² (swŏl′ ō) *n.* A swift-flying bird with long, pointed wings.

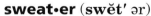

sweat·er (swĕt′ ər) *n.* A knitted garment worn on the upper part of the body.

sweep (swēp) *v.* **swept, sweep·ing.** To clean or clear with a broom or brush: *sweep the floor.*

sweet (swēt) *adj.* **sweet·er, sweet·est. 1.** Having a taste like that of sugar or honey. **2.** Having a pleasant smell: *the sweet smell of flowers.* **3.** Lovable.

swim (swĭm) v. **swam, swum, swim·ming.** To move through the water by using movements of the body.

swoosh (swŏŏsh) or (swōōsh) v. **swooshed, swoosh·ing.** To make a rushing sound: *The water swooshed down the drain.*

take·off (tāk′ ôf′) or (-ŏf) n. The act of leaving the ground in flight: *The takeoff of the airplane was on time.*

taste (tāst) n. **1.** The sense that distinguishes flavor qualities of things placed in the mouth. **2.** A flavor itself: *a sour taste.* —v. **tast·ed, tast·ing.** To distinguish a flavor by taking in the mouth.

taught Look up **teach.**

teach (tēch) v. **taught** (tôt), **teach·ing. 1.** To give instruction: *He teaches math.* **2.** To show how to do: *Tynel taught me how to swim.*

tech·nol·o·gy (tĕk nŏl′ ə jē) n., pl. **tech·nol·o·gies. 1.** The use of science for practical purposes: *Technology is used in developing computers.* **2.** The methods, machines, and materials used in a science or type of work.

teeth Look up **tooth.**

that (thăt) or (thət) adj., pl. **those** (thōz). The one singled out: *that child; that building.*

that's (thăts) Contraction of **that is.**

their (thâr) pron. A possessive form of **they.** Belonging to them: *their dog. These sound alike:* **their, there, they're.**

there (thâr) adv. In or at that place: *The book is over there. These sound alike:* **there, their, they're.**

there·'re (thâr′ ər) Contraction of **there are.**

they'll (thāl) Contraction of **they will.**

they're (thâr) Contraction of **they are.** *These sound alike:* **they're, their, there.**

they've (thāv) Contraction of **they have.**

thick (thĭk) adj. **thick·er, thick·est. 1.** With much space in depth or from side to side: *a thick wall.* **2.** Measuring between two sides: *three feet thick.* **3.** Heavy: *a thick coat of fur.*

thief (thēf) n., pl. **thieves** (thēvz). A person who steals.

think (thĭngk) v. **thought** (thôt), **think·ing. 1.** To form or have in the mind: *think before you act.* **2.** To use the power of reason. **3.** To believe; suppose: *I thought we were lost.*

third (thûrd) adj. Next after second: *the third man at bat.*

those Look up **that.**

though (thō) adv. However; nevertheless: *That doll is pretty; the price is too high, though.*

thought (thôt) n. **1.** The process of thinking. **2.** An idea: *She had some thoughts about decorating the room.*

throat (thrōt) n. The part of the digestive system between the back of the mouth and the esophagus.

through (thrōō) prep. **1.** In one side and out the opposite side of: *through the tunnel.* **2.** Among; in the midst of: *a road through the woods. These sound alike:* **through, threw.**

Thurs·day (thûrz′ dē) or (-dā′) n. The fifth day of the week.

tick·le (tĭk′ əl) v. **tick·led, tick·ling. 1.** To have a tingling sensation. **2.** To touch lightly. **3.** To amuse.

tie (tī) v. **tied, ty·ing. 1.** To fasten with a string or cord: *tie a package.* **2.** To make a bow or knot. **3.** To equal in a contest: *tie the score.* —n. **1.** A cord that ties something. **2.** A necktie. **3.** Equality in scores.

toe (tō) n. One of the five digits at the end of a foot.

to·geth·er (tə gĕth′ ər) adv. **1.** With each other: *Our family was together for Thanksgiving.* **2.** At the same time: *We applauded together.*

toil (toil) v. **toiled, toil·ing.** To work hard for a long time: *Tanya toiled in the garden pulling weeds.* —n. Hard work.

to·mor·row (tə môr′ ō) or (-mŏr′ ō) n. The day after today.

to·night (tə nīt′) *adv.* On or during this night: *It may rain tonight.* —*n.* The night of this day: *Tonight is New Year's Eve.*

too (tōō) *adv.* **1.** Also: *Jim is coming too.* **2.** More than enough: *That bundle is too heavy. These sound alike:* **too, to, two.**

tooth (tōōth) *n., pl.* **teeth** (tēth). Any of the hard, bony structures found in the mouth and set in sockets around the jaw.

tor·ture (tôr′ chər) *v.* **tor·tured, tor·tur·ing.** To cause great pain to someone or something: *Don't torture yourself by worrying too much.* —*n.* **1.** The act of causing severe pain or suffering. **2.** Great pain or suffering: *Speaking in front of the class is torture for some students.*

to·tal (tōt′ l) *n.* **1.** The sum of numbers in addition. **2.** Whole: *The total cost of the car is $5,000.*

touch (tŭch) *v.* **touched, touch·ing. 1.** To come into contact with: *The curtains touch the floor.* **2.** To feel with the hands: *Please don't touch the glass!*

tough (tŭf) *adj.* **tough·er, tough·est. 1.** Strong: *Mules are tough animals.* **2.** Hard to chew: *a tough piece of meat.* **3.** Not easy: *a tough exam.*

to·ward (tôrd) *or* (tə wôrd′) *prep.* **1.** In the direction of: *toward the lake.* **2.** Shortly before; near: *toward evening.*

tow·el (tou′ əl) *n.* A piece of cloth or paper used for wiping or drying.

tow·er (tou′ ər) *n.* A high structure standing alone or forming part of a church, castle, or other building: *The tower rose high in the sky.*

trade (trād) *n.* The business of buying and selling: *trade between countries.* —*v.* **trad·ed, trad·ing. 1.** To engage in buying and selling: *trading with the settlers.* **2.** To exchange: *Serena traded two pieces of gum for the chocolate candy.*

trag·ic (trăj′ ĭk) *adj.* Very sad, unfortunate, or dreadful: *We heard about the tragic accident on the news.*

Pronunciation Key

ă	pat	ŏ	pot	ŭ	cut
ā	pay	ō	toe	ûr	urge
âr	care	ô	paw, for	ə	about,
ä	father	oi	noise		item,
ĕ	pet	ŏŏ	took		edible,
ē	bee	ōō	boot		gallop,
ĭ	pit	ou	out		circus
ī	pie	th	thin	ər	butter
îr	deer	*th*	**th**is		

trail (trāl) *v.* **trailed, trail·ing. 1.** To drag along the ground. **2.** To track: *The police dogs trailed the convict.* —*n.* A path.

trav·el (trăv′ əl) *v.* **trav·eled** or **trav·elled, trav·el·ing** or **trav·el·ling. 1.** To go from one place to another: *travel around the city by bus.* **2.** To be transmitted: *Sound travels through the air.*

trea·son (trē′ zən) *n.* The crime of helping the enemy of a group or country one is loyal to: *Giving plans of attack to the enemy could be considered treason.*

treat (trēt) *v.* **treat·ed, treat·ing. 1.** To act toward: *The judge treated him fairly.* **2.** To provide food or entertainment for: *We were treated to a movie.* —*n.* A source of delight: *The circus was a treat.*

tree (trē) *n., pl.* **trees.** A tall, woody plant with branches and a main stem or trunk.

trou·ble (trŭb′ əl) *n.* **1.** Difficulty: *having trouble unlocking the suitcase.* **2.** A dangerous or difficult situation: *The lost child was in trouble.* **3.** Extra work or effort: *Don't go to any trouble!*

tru·ly (trōō′ lē) *adv.* Sincerely: *I'm truly happy that you're here.*

truth (trōōth) *n.* The real state of a thing; that which is the case: *You should always tell the truth.*

try (trī) *v.* **tried, try·ing. 1.** To sample in order to determine quality: *try the new vacuum cleaner.* **2.** To attempt: *try to run in the marathon.*

Tues·day (tōōz′ dē) *or* (tyōōz′-) *or* (-dā′) *n.* The third day of the week.

twice (twīs) *adv.* Two times: *He has visited San Francisco twice.*

two (tōō) *n.* The number that follows one. *These sound alike:* **two, too, to.**

un·der (ŭn' dər) *prep.* **1.** Below: *under the bed.* **2.** Beneath the surface: *under the sea.* **3.** Less than: *under $5.00.*

un·der·stand (ŭn' dər **stǎnd'**) *v.* **un·der·stood** (ŭn' dər **stōōd'**), **un·der·stand·ing. 1.** To grasp the nature of: *understand science.* **2.** To know thoroughly: *He understands Spanish.* **3.** To realize: *I understand how hard you work at being a good student.*

un·dis·cov·ered (ŭn dĭ **skŭv'** ərd) *adj.* Not found: *Scientists search for undiscovered cures for diseases.*

United States of America (yōō nīt' ĭd stāts ŭv ə **měr'** ĭ kə) *n.* A country in North America consisting of 50 states and the District of Columbia.

u·ni·verse (yōō' nə vûrs') *n.* The whole of existing things, including the earth and all of space.

un·til (ŭn tĭl') *prep.* **1.** Up to the time of: *The awards dinner lasted until 10 o'clock.* **2.** Before: *She won't leave until morning.*

un·time·ly (ŭn tīm' lē) *adj.* **un·time·li·er, un·time·li·est. 1.** Happening at the wrong or improper time: *The girl's untimely sneeze in the play embarrassed her.* **2.** Happening too soon: *The untimely blooming of the flowers was due to the mild winter.*

up·stairs (ŭp' stârz') *adv.* Up the stairs. —*n.* The upper floor.

U·ra·nus (yōōr' ə nəs) *or* (yōō rā'-) *n.* The seventh planet of the solar system in increasing distance from the sun.

u·ten·sil (yōō tĕn' səl) *n., pl.* **u·ten·sils.** A tool or object that is useful for making or doing something: *Knives and forks are utensils used for eating.*

var·nish (vär' nĭsh) *n., pl.* **var·nish·es.** A liquid-like paint that gives a thin, hard, clear surface.

vast·ness (văst' nəs) *or* (-nĭs) *n.* Greatness in area or size; hugeness: *The vastness of the ocean is amazing.*

Ve·nus (vē' nəs) *n.* The second planet of the solar system in increasing distance from the sun.

vil·lage (vĭl' ĭj) *n.* A group of houses that form a community, usually smaller than a town.

voice (vois) *n.* Sounds made by the respiratory system that come through the mouth: *Her voice was loud and raspy.*

vol·can·ic (vŏl kǎn' ĭk) *or* (vôl-) *adj.* Of or produced by a volcano: *When the volcano exploded, there was volcanic ash everywhere.*

vow·el (vou' əl) *n.* **1.** A voiced speech sound produced by not blocking the breath. **2.** A letter that represents a sound, such as *a, e, i, o,* or *u.*

voy·age (voi' ĭj) *n.* A long journey made by a ship or sometimes by an aircraft or spacecraft.

waist (wāst) *n.* The part of the human body between the ribs and the hips. *These sound alike:* **waist, waste.**

wait (wāt) *v.* **wait·ed, wait·ing.** To stay or stop doing something until someone or something comes: *Wait until the plane lands. These sound alike:* **wait, weight.**

wal·let (wŏl' ĭt) *n.* A small, flat case for holding paper money, coins, photographs, etc.

wan·der (wŏn' dər) *v.* **wan·dered, wan·der·ing.** To travel from place to place freely; roam: *wander around the shopping mall.*

warm (wôrm) *adj.* **warm·er, warm·est.** Moderately hot; having some heat: *warm water; warm weather.*

wash (wŏsh) *or* (wôsh) *v.* **washed, wash·ing. 1.** To clean with water and often soap: *wash your hands.* **2.** To be removed or carried by moving water: *High tide washed away the seashells.* —*n.* A batch of clothes that are to be or have just been washed.

was·n't (wŏz' ənt) *or* (wŭz'-) Contraction of **was not.**

waste (wāst) *v.* **wast·ed, wast·ing.** To spend or use up foolishly: *He wasted his money on that awful movie! These sound alike:* **waste, waist.**

watch (wŏch) *v.* **watched, watch·ing. 1.** To look at: *Watch the birds in flight!* **2.** To be on the lookout: *Watch for falling rocks!* —*n.* A small timepiece worn on the wrist or on a chain.

wa·ter (wô' tər) *or* (wŏt' ər) *n.* A liquid made up of hydrogen and oxygen that covers three fourths of the earth's surface. —*v.* **wa·tered, wa·ter·ing.** To sprinkle or moisten with water.

weath·er (wĕ*th*' ər) *n.* The condition of the atmosphere with regard to temperature, moisture, wind, etc.

Wednes·day (wĕnz' dē) *or* (-dā') *n.* The fourth day of the week.

week·end (wēk' ĕnd') *n.* The end of the week, especially the time from Friday evening to Sunday evening.

weight (wāt) *n.* **1.** The force with which a body is attracted to the earth or other celestial bodies: *Our weight is less on the moon.* **2.** How heavy a thing is: *The baby's weight is 16 pounds. These sound alike:* **weight, wait.**

we're (wîr) Contraction of **we are.**

weren't (wûrnt) *or* (wûr' ənt) Contraction of **were not.**

where (wâr) *adv.* At or in what place: *Where is the dog?*

wheth·er (wĕ*th*' ər) *conj.* **1.** Used to express two choices: *whether to walk or drive.* **2.** If: *I asked whether I should wash the chalkboard.*

Pronunciation Key

ă	pat	ŏ	pot	ŭ	cut
ā	pay	ō	toe	ûr	urge
âr	care	ô	paw, for	ə	about,
ä	father	oi	noise		item,
ĕ	pet	ŏŏ	took		edible,
ē	bee	ōō	boot		gallop,
ĭ	pit	ou	out		circus
ī	pie	th	thin	ər	butter
îr	deer	*th*	*th*is		

whis·tle (wĭs' əl) *v.* **whis·tled, whis·tling.** To make a clear, high-pitched sound by forcing breath through the teeth or by pursing the lips. —*n.* Instrument used for whistling.

wife (wīf) *n., pl.* **wives** (wīvz) A woman to whom a man is married.

will (wĭl) *aux. v.* **would** (wŏŏd) **1.** Used to indicate future action or condition: *They will go bowling tonight.* **2.** Used to indicate certainty: *You will see me again.*

win (wĭn) *v.* **won** (wŭn), **win·ning. 1.** To achieve victory over others: *win a game.* **2.** To receive an award for performance: *She won the Nobel Prize for her research in science.*

win·dow (wĭn' dō) *n.* **1.** An opening in a wall to let in light or air. **2.** A pane of glass.

win·ter (wĭn' tər) *n.* The season of the year between autumn and spring.

wise (wīz) *adj.* **wis·er, wis·est. 1.** Having wisdom or good judgment. **2.** Showing common sense.

with·out (wĭ*th* out') *or* (wĭ*th*-) *prep.* Not having; lacking: *without money; without food.*

wives Look up **wife.**

wolf (wŏŏlf) *n., pl.* **wolves** (wŏŏlvz). A flesh-eating animal related to the dog.

wom·an (wŏŏm' ən) *n., pl.* **wom·en** (wĭm' ĭn). An adult female person.

wom·en Look up **woman.**

won Look up **win.**

won·der·ful (wŭn′ dər fəl) *adj.* Marvelous; remarkable: *a wonderful trip.*

won·drous (wŭn′ drəs) *adj.* Remarkable; marvelous: *A rainbow in the desert is a wondrous sight.*

wood·en (wŏŏd′ n) *adj.* Made of wood: *a wooden table.*

wool (wŏŏl) *n.* The soft, curly fur of sheep, used for yarn and clothing.

world (wûrld) *n.* **1.** The earth. **2.** All of certain parts, people, or things of the world: *the sports world; the animal world.*

worth·while (wûrth′ wīl′) *adj.* Important enough to be worth the time, effort, or money spent: *Reading a good book is worthwhile.*

would Look up **will.**

would·n't (wŏŏd′ nt) Contraction of **would not.**

wrin·kle (rĭng′ kəl) *n.* A small ridge or crease on a normally smooth surface. —*v.* **wrin·kled, wrin·kling.** To make wrinkles in: *Don't wrinkle the paper.*

write (rīt) *v.* **wrote** (rōt), **writ·ten** (rĭt′ n), **writ·ing. 1.** To form letters on a surface with a pen or pencil. **2.** To compose and record on paper.

wrong (rông) *or* (rŏng) *adj.* **1.** Not correct: *a wrong answer.* **2.** Contrary to morality or law: *Lying is wrong.*

yawn (yôn) *v.* **yawned, yawn·ing.** To open the mouth wide and take in air when sleepy.

yd Abbreviation for **yard.**

yes·ter·day (yĕs′ tər dā′) *or* (-dē) *n.* The day before today.

you'd (yŏŏd) **1.** Contraction of **you had. 2.** Contraction of **you would.**

yours (yŏŏrz) *or* (yôrz) *pron.* A possessive form of **you.** Used to indicate that something belongs to you: *That book is yours.*

ze·bra (zē′ brə) *n.* An African animal related to the horse.

ze·ro (zîr′ ō) *or* (zē′ rō) *n., pl.* **ze·ros** or **ze·roes. 1.** The numerical symbol 0. **2.** The temperature on a scale indicated by this symbol.